THE
WINE CURMUDGEON'S
GUIDE TO *Cheap Wine*

THE
WINE CURMUDGEON'S
GUIDE TO *Cheap Wine*

JEFF SIEGEL

*For DnA –
Enjoy what
you drink,
& and drink
what you enjoy*

Vintage Noir Media
Dallas, Texas

Printed in the United States of America
First Printing, 2013

ISBN 978-0-9897190-0-1
ISBN 978-0-9897190-1-8 (ebook)

Vintage Noir Media
6646 Aintree Circle
Dallas, Texas 75214
www.vintage-noir.com

As I ate the oysters with their strong taste of the sea and their faint metallic taste that the cold white wine washed away, leaving only the sea taste and the succulent texture, and as I drank their cold liquid from each shell and washed it down with the crisp taste of the wine, I lost the empty feeling and began to be happy and to make plans.

—Ernest Hemingway, *A Moveable Feast*

Contents

The 10-point
quick start guide
to cheap wine

The book's five chapters and the Other Good Stuff to Know section aren't complicated. Each offers direct, clear-cut advice and background to help you understand each step in buying, drinking, and enjoying cheap wine. Read them, and you're that much closer to having the tools to figure out wine for yourself — without consulting scores of dubious provenance; without consulting an "expert" to tell you what to drink; and without any of the other foolishness that passes for wine education. Learning about wine means learning the process that leads to satisfying results, and the ultimate satisfying result is finding cheap wine that you like and finding it on your own. This book is about that process.

That's one reason why there aren't any wine recommendations in the book. That won't help you learn how to do it yourself (though you can consult the Wine Curmudgeon's annual $10 Hall of Fame, which appears every January on the blog, or any of the blog's reviews). In addition, wine is ever-changing. What may be a great cheap wine when the book is written may not be a great cheap wine when you read this; hence the link to the Hall of Fame and the blog; and, more importantly, the need to learn how to find great cheap wine on your own.

This quick start guide outlines the process, covering 10 of the most important points that the book discusses over the next 134 pages. Use the links to go directly to the part of the book that explains that concept.

1. Price is not always a function of quality, and a $100 wine is not always 10 times better than a $10 wine. page 9

2. The best wine is wine that you like. If you don't like it, don't drink it. Do you eat chocolate ice cream because someone tells you to, even if you don't like chocolate ice cream? page 101

3. The only way to learn about wine, and to find out what you like, is to drink wine — just like the only way to learn how to drive a car is to drive a car. page 52

4. You don't have to like all the wine you drink — and it's OK to say you don't like it. page 53

5. Don't be afraid to try something different. There are an almost infinite number of wines in the world, and much of the fun with wine is exploring. page 128

6. Cute labels and a funny name do not make a quality wine, just as a fancy name and serious label do not make a quality wine. page 46

7. Wine and food pairings, no matter how well-intentioned, are just suggestions. page 95

8. A quality retailer who can help you find wine that you like is invaluable. page 69

9. Wine scores are one person's opinion, and mean very little if that person likes wine that you don't. Wine score essay, page 123

10. Wine is supposed to be fun, and you don't have to pay any attention to anything that gets in the way of having fun. Introduction, page 5

INTRODUCTION

Why cheap wine matters

I was once a wine snob. I drank what other people told me to drink, I thought what other people told me to think, and I knew — without having to taste it — if a wine was any good.

I was 23, though, and had tasted maybe a dozen glasses in my life. So at least I had an excuse.

Which is more than too many of the country's wine drinkers have. We can argue about the popularity of wine in the United States. We can argue about whether wine is part of the French paradox and boosts heart health. We can even argue about whether wine should have corks or screwcaps (though you can probably guess where I stand).

But the one thing that's as indisputable as it is depressing is that there are only two kinds of wine drinkers in this country — the snobs and everyone else. And, since the snobs run the wine business, the rest of us are left to fend for ourselves. What makes a good wine? How much should wine cost? What's the difference between cabernet sauvignon and merlot? Who knows? Why should we know? It's certainly not easy to find by consulting what I call the Winestream Media — the wine magazines, websites, and blogs whose writers and columnists dominate wine coverage in the U.S. and whose goal is more often to reinforce wine's stereo-types than to educate wine drinkers. They'll tell you about wine as an investment, as if it was real estate; wax poetic about cult wines from producers who make so little that it's impossible to buy, even if you could afford it; and categorize every wine they review on the infamous 100-point scale, which reduces wine to dollar signs and decimal points so you can try to decide if an 89-point wine that costs $40 is a better value than 90-point wine that costs $50.

This helps explain why, in the second decade of the 21st century, despite every single advance wine has made in this country since the 1970s — the French paradox, improved wine quality, better availability, six times the number of wineries as in 1975, and even the aforementioned screwcaps — Americans, on a per capita basis, still drank three times as much beer as wine and twice as much hard liquor as wine, according to the National Institute on Alcohol Abuse and Alcoholism. Consumption per person has been the same for almost three decades, says the Wine Institute trade group — about one bottle of wine per adult each month. And, as the Wine Market Council has noted, just 20 percent or so of adult Americans drink 9 out of every 10 bottles of wine sold in the U.S.

That's why I was anointed the Wine Curmudgeon more than a decade ago by the food editor at the Star-Telegram newspaper in Forth Worth, Texas. My job, then as now — to speak for the ordi-nary wine drinker, to stand up for everyone who is overwhelmed by wine's confusion, and to be as curmudgeonly as possible in defense of cheap wine and the value and enjoyment it brings.

Why me? First, because I brought a consumer sensibility to wine writing that was then missing (and still isn't as common as it should be). I was trained as a newspaperman, which meant I wrote for readers and not to prove I was smarter than they were. That meant using clear language, avoiding jargon, and offering practical advice that they could use to buy wine that was available and affordable. It didn't mean waxing poetic, dropping names, cadging free samples, and writing about wine that was too expensive or that they couldn't buy. Second, I learned to love wine without any other training than drinking it, paying attention, and drinking some more. I was a Chicago beer drinker who didn't grow up with wine, save for my father's Bolla Valpolicella, a staple in certain types of 1970s suburban homes. I knew what consumers wanted because I was one of them.

And that's fun, the way the very fine Southern novelist Clyde Edgerton described it in "Raney," a book about the marriage of an Atlanta Episcopalian, Charles, and a rural Baptist, Raney. Toward the end of the book, Raney, who doesn't drink, discovers wine. And her discovery rings true:

> . . . Charles has got me to sip his white wine at the Ramada a few times — to show me how much better it makes the food taste. One night I tried a whole glass. Just to make the food taste better, because it can make the food taste some better, depending on what you're eating. Thursday night, when we stopped by the store I'd had *two* glasses. For the first time. I don't think I'll ever do it again, and I shouldn't have then. I can't decide what I think about it exactly. It does make the food taste some better.

Raney opens her mind, and wine starts to make sense to her. Wine is fun. Wine is enjoyable. Wine isn't complicated. Wine is sharing a glass at the Ramada, and it almost doesn't matter what kind of wine it is or who makes it and it certainly doesn't matter what its score is. The late wine writer Darryl Beeson always insisted that the best wines weren't necessarily the "best" wines, but wines that were part of an important experience — first date, birth of child, long-awaited vacation. In this, the wine depended as much on who you were with and where you were when you drank it as to what it tasted like. In which case, a $3 bottle of wine from a 7-Eleven bought on the spur of the moment on the way to a watch movies on the sofa could be as much fun as the 99-point, $300 wine served in a high-end restaurant by a corps of fawning waiters. Or even more fun, if the truth be known.

This is a distinctly European approach to wine, where wine is not about special occasions and people don't wait for a wine critic to approve of what they drink. Wine is on the table every night at dinner, as much a part of the meal as plates and silverware. Even today, when wine drinking has declined across Europe and a variety of commentators have written long and questioning pieces about the end of the European wine tradition, the world's biggest consumers of wine, on a per capita basis, include the French, Italians and Portuguese, each of whom drink about five times as much as Americans.

To be fair, the Europeans have a bit of a head start on us. They've been drinking wine for 4,000 years; in the 12th century, one reason Henry II of England married Eleanor of Aquitaine was because her dowry included Bordeaux — then as now, one of the most important wine-producing regions in the world. That head start has mostly to do with two things: agriculture and dysentery. First, continental Europe south of Germany is ideal for growing the grapes that are easiest to turn into the best quality wines — *vitis vinifera*, for those who are inclined toward Latin and which most people know as the genus and species of the best-known grape varieties like chardonnay, cabernet sauvignon, and merlot. Second, wine was safer to drink than water for 3,800 years, and remained so until the Industrial Revolution in the middle of the 19th century brought with it modern sanitation. Wine, which is fermented, is disease-free. So why not drink it at every meal?

In the U.S., on the other hand, the modern wine business dates only to the end of World War II. Americans drank beer and rum, and later whiskey; in 1860, the typical American adult drank

2 gallons of spirits a year (the equivalent of some 200 cocktails), or about 20 times the amount of wine they drank. The fledgling U.S. wine industry that was destroyed by Prohibition never really grabbed hold of the U.S. drinking public. For one thing, *vinifera* was difficult to grow in the U.S. outside of California before the last decades of the 20th century, and the centers of the U.S. wine industry in the 19th century were Ohio, near Cincinnati, and Missouri, not California. The grains used to make beer and spirits, on the other hand, are the corn and wheat that thrive almost anywhere in the U.S. So, in those days before modern supply chains and high-speed transport, when it was almost as difficult to ship Missouri wine in New York City as French wine, people drank local, and local meant beer and spirits. In this, the American attitude toward wine didn't start to change until the end of World War II, when GIs who had fought in Europe and had seen wine first-hand became the first group of Americans to appreciate wine.

But not enough. See if you can guess when this was written:

> And in the past five years we have hardly seen any real *vin ordinaire* (by which I mean a common, *inexpensive* table wine) sold in America. The humble gallon jug virtually disappeared . . . from our wine merchants' shelves; instead, the undistinguished reds and whites from the mass production areas of California appeared in fancy dress at a fancy price, and elaborate advertising campaigns were launched to convince us that bottles which we used to buy reluctantly . . . were suddenly worth [2 ½ times as much and] being sold us as a special favor.

That's not a 21st century Wine Curmudgeon rant. It was written in 1947 by Frank Schoonmaker, one of the first great U.S. wine critics. Isn't it time we finally changed this attitude? Haven't we been waiting too long? The answer to both questions is yes, and the time is now.

Chapter I

Cheap wine's long and winding road

Wine drinkers know something is up. They're just not quite sure what to do about it. Or, as one reader told the editor of a South African newspaper:

> Your wine columnist continues to opine in his quaint, elitist style, as if anyone who can't afford a bottle at (US$21), or was it (US$210), is beneath him. Many wine writers give the impression that nothing below a certain price point will ever contaminate their nostrils, let alone their lips.

That's because more and more wine drinkers understand something that the critics and bloggers and columnists in the Winestream Media don't: That wine doesn't have to cost a lot of money to be enjoyable. Call it cheap. Call it inexpensive. Call it value wine. But whatever you call it, it doesn't have to be expensive. Just $10 — and often less — will buy a perfectly acceptable and often excellent bottle of wine. The wine could be from California, but it could just as easily be from the Pacific Northwest, France, Spain, Italy, Australia, New Zealand, or South America. It could be made with grapes that many of us have heard of, or with grapes that are as difficult to pronounce as they are uncommon. Just because it's difficult to say "viognier" doesn't mean it can't be turned into great cheap wine.

All the wine drinker needs is the courage of his or her convictions, the curiosity to try wine they aren't familiar with, and enough education so they can make sense of the latter — because that will allow them to do the former.

It's that simple, no matter what anyone else says. We don't think less of people because they drink cheap orange juice. So why do we assume they're somehow inferior if they drink cheap wine?

2,200 years of wine

The irony is that everyone else in the world has long known this. Roman peasants were drinking inexpensive wine 2,200 years ago, while the daily wine ration of cheap *pinard* helped the French *poilu* endure the mud and grime and slaughter of the First World War trenches.

It's only in places like the U.S., where there isn't an obvious and acknowledged history of wine that wine is seen as something that's a bit above most people. How many times have you heard someone start a conversation about wine — or started one yourself — with the dreaded phrase, "I'm not an expert. . . ."? Does anyone do that when they talk about ketchup?

But we do about wine. We suffer in silence. We assume our betters know better. Ask an American about football, and they'll have an opinion, and it doesn't matter if the only thing they know about the game is that each team has 11 players. Ask them about politics, and they'll have an opinion, and it doesn't matter whether they vote or aren't sure who the vice president is.

Ask them about wine, on the other hand, and you'll get a blank stare. "It's too complicated," they'll say. Or, "That's too fancy for me. I drink beer." Or, my favorite, "I don't know wine. What do you think I should drink?"

A short history of cheap wine

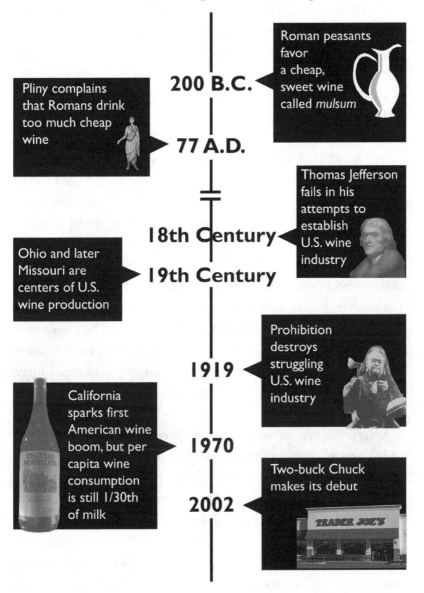

Roman peasants favor a cheap, sweet wine called *mulsum*

200 B.C.

Pliny complains that Romans drink too much cheap wine

77 A.D.

Thomas Jefferson fails in his attempts to establish U.S. wine industry

18th Century

19th Century

Ohio and later Missouri are centers of U.S. wine production

Prohibition destroys struggling U.S. wine industry

1919

California sparks first American wine boom, but per capita wine consumption is still 1/30th of milk

1970

Two-buck Chuck makes its debut

2002

This attitude is as old as the American wine industry, which, in fits and starts, moved from the Ohio River Valley around Cincinnati before the Civil War to Missouri in the last decades of the 19th century and then to California before Prohibition. The author and critic Todd Kliman has argued that Victorian-era Americans saw wine as something foreign, a business run by people with hard to pronounce last names who, even if not recent immigrants, still really weren't Americans. So why would a real American want to buy their product?

That snobbishness extended to wine's first success in the U.S., the boom in California that saw production increase five-fold in the 30 years or so before Prohibition. But it came as part of a cartel called the California Wine Association, formed by seven wineries to set prices at the expense of growers and consumers and to guarantee themselves profit. Or, as the the wine critic Paul Lukacs wrote of the cartel's organizer, an Englishman named Percy Morgan: He "did not much care who drank the wines, or what kind of wines they drank. His goal above all else was profit, and he clearly realized it." Though, in the end, the boom wasn't even all that much of a boom — in 1910, the average American drank 10 times more beer than wine, and most of the wine they did drink was imported from Europe.

Americans just weren't all that interested in wine. The Hayes Office, which censored the movies from the 1930s to the 1960s, regularly enforced its Rule No. 4: "The use of liquor in American life, when not required by the plot or for proper characterization, will not be shown." So much for having a glass of wine with dinner. And it's probably not a coincidence that when the censors did allow liquor in a movie, it wasn't wine. Nick and Nora Charles spend most of the movie version of "The Thin Man" getting drunk on Prohibition-era cocktails. In 1955, a Roper survey found that "wine is not regarded as a familiar part of American life" and wine drinking was an "old world custom."

How the three-tier system works
Each tier can only buy from the tier above it

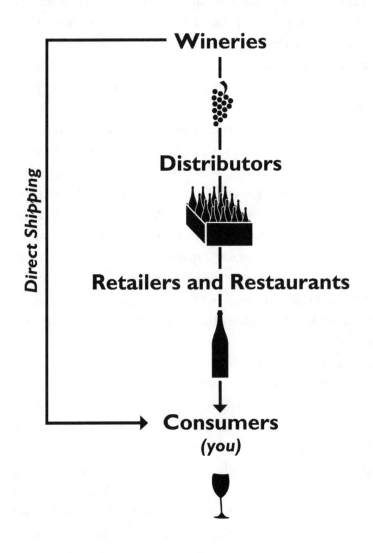

Wineries

Distributors

Retailers and Restaurants

Direct Shipping

Consumers
(you)

Prohibition is still with us

To be fair, Prohibition — the 18th Amendment to the U.S. Constitution, which took effect in 1920 and which outlawed the sale, manufacture, and transportation of alcohol in the U.S. until it was repealed in 1933 by the 21st Amendment — played an important role in the formation of that attitude. And it still does. Why else do almost two dozen states still restrict the sale of alcohol in one way or another, whether with dry counties, price controls, or a ban on Sunday sales? And wine drinkers suffer under the three-tier system, perhaps Prohibition's greatest legacy.

The political compromise that ended Prohibition allowed each state to regulate alcohol in its own way, and they have — in ways that are completely unimaginable. New Yorkers can't buy wine in grocery stores. Montgomery County, Md., residents can't buy wine at retailers like Cost Plus World Market, but residents of adjacent Prince George's County can. There are not just 50 laws for 50 states, but laws that vary from county to county within states, and even — get ready for this — different laws within the same city. Retailers in two-thirds of Dallas can only sell beer and wine, while those in the other third can sell beer, wine and spirits.

The three-tier system, which is used by each state in some form or another, requires wineries, breweries and distilleries to sell their product to a distributor. The distributor can only sell alcohol to the retailer or restaurant, and the consumer can only buy alcohol from the retailer or restaurant. The only exceptions? Buying wine if you're actually at the winery and what's called direct shipping — where, if the state you live in allows it, you can buy wine from an out-of-state winery, which will ship it to your home. But only about a dozen or so states permit direct shipping.

This makes wine different from almost every other consumer good in the world. If you want to buy a computer from Dell or shoes from Nike, each is only a couple of mouse clicks away. And Amazon has become a $61 billion company by serving as the ultimate retailer, able to cross state lines to serve its customers. But ordering wine from an out-of-state producer is a crime in much of the U.S., and it's a crime in every state to order wine from an out-of-state retailer. On-line retailers like Wine.com, which is in 42 states, have to legally qualify as an in-state wine retailer (by setting up an office or a warehouse, for example) to be allowed to do business in those states.

But, all of that, as bad as it is, is not the worst part about three-tier. The worst part is that three-tier limits consumer choice. Do you live in Illinois and had a wine you liked at dinner in Wisconsin? Did you try to buy that wine in Illinois only to find that it isn't available? That's the fault of three-tier. Remember, every wine sold to a retailer or restaurant has to come through a distributor, but just because a distributor in Wisconsin carries the wine is no guarantee that a distributor in Illinois will carry it. The Illinois distributor may not like the wine or the person who makes it or how much it costs. So they decide not to carry it, and you can't buy it — even though it's available in another state just a half-hour drive away.

This is an especially acute problem for cheap wine. Distributors, all things being equal, prefer to deal with the biggest producers. They can get better pricing, the supply chain is more efficient, there is money for marketing, and they'll have more wine to sell since big producers deal in tens of thousands of cases. But much cheap wine — perhaps the most interesting cheap wine — is made by smaller companies that don't produce tens of thousands of cases, can't offer the best prices, have less efficient delivery systems, and whose wines are more quirky. So they have more difficulty finding a distributor — and often can't. This is such a problem that there are trade events for wineries that don't have distributors, held in the hope that a distributor will sample their wines and then take them on. It's kind of sad, actually. Meanwhile, smaller wineries that do have distributors usually have to settle for smaller distributors that have less clout with retailers, which means the producer's wines are limited in availability and may even cost more.

The other annoying thing about three-tier? It's constitutionally protected in the U.S., just like freedom of speech and freedom of religion. The Supreme Court has ruled, as recently as 2005, that the 21st Amendment shelters three-tier from court challenges and state and federal legislation. So we're stuck with it.

Affordable luxury

If Prohibition is known today, it's for three-tier and gangsters like Al Capone. What's forgotten is that it was known as the Noble Experiment, a social reform with roots in 19th-century political and social groups like the Anti-Saloon League, the Prohibition Party, and the Women's Christian Temperance Union. They saw alcohol as the cause of many of the problems that came with urbanization and the Industrial Revolution — drunkenness, broken homes, and increased violence. Even some of the Progressives, an important 19th-century political movement that wanted to outlaw child labor, give women the vote, and reform the economy, endorsed Prohibition.

Yet there were darker, less wholesome motives at work. As the U.S. changed from an agrarian to an urban society in the 19th century, there were increasing attempts by the dry movement to equate alcohol with sin, and to tar the people who drank — the wets — as sinners who had to be saved from themselves. The drys were often rural, fundamentalist Protestants who resented the social changes that accompanied urbanization and the Industrial Revolution. So if alcohol was consumed in big city taverns and saloons, and if the saloons were frequented by German,

Italian, and Irish immigrants who were mostly Catholic, then all would be well if the U.S. banned alcohol. Also not surprising: The 10 states that didn't ratify the 21st Amendment, which repealed Prohibition, were farming states mostly without big cities.

Given this idea of liquor as sin, it's not too far a leap to where we are today — the culmination of a phenomenon that the wine economist Rob McMillan has described as "mass luxury." Wine, he has written, "is positioned as more of a luxury or a lifestyle enhancement, even in the lower price points." Ordinary people don't drink wine. Only the elite, who aren't afraid of sin and who are comfortable with something that's defined as a luxury, drink wine.

In other words, how can luxury only cost $10?

It can't, and this contradiction is at the heart of the wine business. Too many in the wine business, whether producer, distributor, retailer, or writer, treat wine as a luxury product. They use luxury terms to sell it, describe it, and criticize it. The Winestream Media, and especially its glossy, high-end magazines, push not only expensive wine but luxury cars, vacation travel, and $100 per person restaurants. It's no surprise that a Wine Spectator columnist wrote in 2012, and in all seriousness, that democratizing wine was a lousy idea, calling it the "biggest lie of them all."

The most obvious, and most aggravating, example of this are descriptors — the adjectives used to describe what wine tastes like, and which turn up in things called tasting notes. Tasting notes are short, two- or three-sentence reviews of wine, and you'll rarely see simple terms like fruity, sweet, clean, or fresh. Instead, tasting notes feature descriptors that are dense, complicated and often nonsensical, running the gamut from "redolent of leather and tobacco" to, as hard as it is to believe, "liquefied Viagra."

The reason for all this is as obvious as it is depressing: Language is power. If we can't figure out what they're talking about, they're smarter than we are, and we have to accept their wisdom. As the critic W. Blake Gray has written: "I imagined the average wine consumer . . . seeing, 'This wine tastes like blackberry, vanilla and peach galette.' But I couldn't imagine her reaction. Does she think, 'Mmm, that sounds good!'? Does she think, 'I never taste these flavors, but the people who write these are professionals so the fault is mine'? "

At first, these descriptors were mostly used for expensive wine, but they're used for all wines now, no matter what the price. So it's not uncommon for a $10 red wine to boast about its licorice-like flavors, which is rarely possible given the quality of the grapes used to make $10 wine — and quite off-putting, too, if the person writing the descriptor stopped to think about it. Licorice, indeed. Who wants to drink a wine that tastes like those long, leathery strands of candy that kids eat?

Yet, if you look at the numbers, wine long ago stopped being a luxury product in the way that most of us think of luxury. Who can buy diamond rings at the grocery store? But you can buy lots and lots of wine — almost too much, as anyone who has rushed into a supermarket on the way home from work to buy a bottle for dinner has noticed. Six companies sell almost two-thirds of the wine in the U.S., accounting for almost 250 brands. That's hardly a Gucci experience.

We buy cheap wine

Sales statistics tell the same story. The average price of wine sold in the U.S. was less than $7 in 2011, reported Nielsen, while 9 out of 10 bottles of wine sold that year cost less than $12 and one out of every four bottles cost less than $3. The last percentage has fallen by about half over the past 20 years, but we are still — overwhelmingly — a country that appreciates cheap wine. How else to explain the growth, over the last five years, of a new category of wine known as value or ultra-cheap and that sells for $3

$3

One out of four bottles of wine sold in the U.S. costs less than $3

$7
The average price of a bottle of wine in the U.S.

90% < $12

90% of wine sold in the U.S. costs less than $12

Above statistics according to Nielsen, 2012

According to informal Wine Curmudgeon poll

$20 The average price of a bottle of wine, according to consumers or $4? These are professionally made wines that aren't necessarily sweet or flawed, which would have been the case a decade ago (examples of which still exist in boxed wines like Almaden and Franzia, which sell for the equivalent of $2 or $3 a bottle). These value brands include Trader Joe's Two-buck Chuck, Walmart's Oak Leaf, Whole Foods' Three Wishes, and 7-Eleven's Yosemite Road—all sold by successful, profitable companies that usually don't do things that don't make money. Two-buck Chuck, which got its nickname because it cost $1.99 a bottle when it debuted in 2002 under the Charles Shaw name, sold more than 50 million cases in its first decade. That probably makes Charles Shaw, which is owned by the Bronco Wine Co. (one of the Big Six noted above) among the 30 biggest producers in the U.S.—if it was an actual producer. The Whole Foods brand, given the company's upscale and better-educated demographics, may be even more intriguing, because it means that the same people who are willing to pay the Whole Foods premium for organic vegetables and free-range poultry also want to buy $4 wine.

The most important thing to know about wine pricing is that it's a function of real estate—the more expensive the land means the more expensive the grapes, and so the more the wine will cost. This is a generalization, certainly, and there are exceptions, and especially in Europe. But for most of the wine that most of us drink, the cost of land matters. Prime vineyard locations in Napa Valley can cost as much as $300,000 an acre. By comparison, the cost in Sonoma County—generally regarded as the second-best wine region in California—ran between $60,000 and $140,000 an acre in 2011. In Mendocino, not as well known as Napa or Sonoma but still a quality region, prices were about one-quarter of Napa; in the Central Valley, where the grapes come from for jug and value wines, land prices are a fraction of Mendocino.

The cost of a bottle of wine

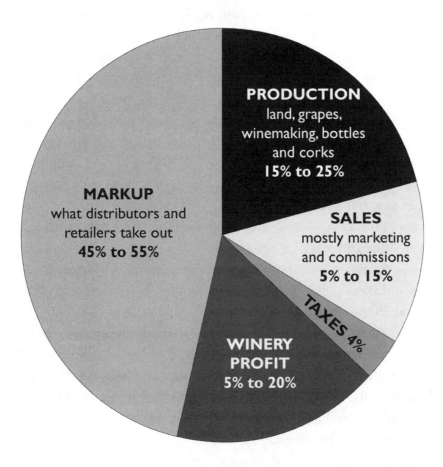

This is one reason why it's so difficult to get a handle on the relationship between pricing and quality. Expensive land doesn't necessarily translate into the best wine, but since producers have to account for their costs, it does translate into expensive wine. If they overpaid for their land, consumers have to make up the difference without getting any additional value.

That's why determining the cost breakdown of a bottle of wine is so difficult to do: how much does each part of the process, from land to bottle to labor, cost? A Big Six producer, which uses Central Valley grapes and can take advantage of economies of scale that smaller producers don't have, has a completely different breakdown than a Napa producer. On the other hand, marketing costs for less expensive wines are probably much higher than those for Napa wines, which have limited production and face less competition. Get a 98 from a wine magazine, and you don't have to spend anything on marketing at all. Having said all that, this economic breakdown, put together from interviews with producers of varying sizes, should be reasonably accurate:

- Production — land, grapes, winemaking, packaging, bottles and corks: 15 to 25 percent
- Sales — mostly marketing and commissions: 5 to 15 percent
- Taxes — 4 percent
- Profit — 5 to 20 percent
- Markup — what distributors and retailers take out: 45 to 55 percent

In other words, the winery could make as little as 50 cents on a $10 bottle of wine, while more than half of the $10 goes to the distributor and retailer. Is it any wonder that distributors are so enamored of the three-tier system?

Understanding the contradiction

That the distributor makes more on a bottle of wine than the winery is just another of the contradictions that make up the wine business. Which also raises the next question: Why does the wine business approach wine in a way that is completely different from the way most wine drinkers approach it? Much of it is tradition — the wine business has always worked one way, and change is difficult. Some of the most important developments in the consumer goods business over the past decade passed the wine business by, and no one seemed to notice (or even care that much). Hispanic marketing has been crucial for companies like Procter & Gamble and Coke and retailers like Walmart (its CEO has said that 100 percent of the growth in the retailer's sales will come from multicultural customers) since at least the 2000 census, which found that the Hispanic population had increased 61 percent since 1990. But wine drinkers remain overwhelmingly white, reports the Wine Market Council, making up 80 percent of the council's core wine consumer (who drink the most wine the most often). Hispanics, meanwhile, make up only five percent of the core consumer group even though they're 13 percent of the U.S. population. That's impossible to believe at a time when Hispanic households in the U.S. that earn $50,000 or more are growing at a faster rate than total households and when most experts expect the U.S. to be a minority majority country by 2050. Said an official of a grape growers trade group: "We really have not done a good job of translating our product to that demographic. Given the growth of the Hispanic segment of the market, it seems apropos that we find out what these folks want to drink."

But it's not only Hispanics to whom the wine business has difficulty marketing. The recent and incredible growth in sweet red wine and moscato, which happened almost by accident, demonstrates how set in its ways the business can be. This is not a discussion about sweet quality or whether it's OK to drink sweet; rather, that the industry has been making sweet wine for decades but never thought much about it. Sweet red in particular was the province of regional wine, all those little wineries in weird places like Texas and New York and Virginia, and so was always seen as beneath the biggest and most legitimate producers in California. But then Gallo released a sweet red called Apothic five years ago, and it launched what has became the hottest category in the wine business. How big? Bigger than sauvignon blanc and syrah/shiraz and almost bigger than pinot grigio, according to national sales figures from one of the largest distributors in the country, totaling almost $300 million in sales in 2012 in grocery stores and warehouse clubs. That was six times as much as white zinfandel, the wine industry's previous sweet effort and one that it was mostly ashamed of.

What's most interesting about sweet red, though, aren't the numbers. It's the frenzy that followed after the rest of the business saw Apothic's success and launched dozens and dozens of other sweet reds. Here was a product that anyone could have done, but didn't — until another company proved that it worked. This does not speak highly of the wine business' understanding of what its customers want or that it even wants to know what they want. It's probably not a coincidence that, when sweet reds hit the market with such a flourish, Steve Heimoff, one of the leading members of the Winestream Media, wrote: "The sweet red wine trend will pick up steam, but who cares?"

The other reason that the wine industry doesn't change is that it doesn't have to, thanks to the constitutionally-protected three-tier system. For the most part, it's still doing business like it did before World War II. Yes, distributors and retailers have computers and most of the rest of the necessary 21st century trappings, and the wineries make better wine than ever before using the latest technology. But the product is still sold the way it was 70 years ago. This would be unthinkable in almost any other industry, but in wine it's considered normal, and those of us who question it are considered troublemakers.

Think of the advantages this brings to the distributors, wineries and retailers — costs are contained, because companies know exactly what they can and can't do to sell product, and competition is reduced, because consumers can only buy wine one way. Nothing illustrates this better than wine prices at the winery that makes the wine, which should theoretically be cheaper than at a retailer. If nothing else, there isn't any transportation to pay for. But the price is usually the same as at retail (if not more, which is another story). That's because the winery doesn't want to offend its distributor by undercutting it on price.

This doesn't mean that every retailer and every winery supports three-tier or doesn't want it to change. The biggest retailers, like Costco, Walmart, and the national grocery store chains, want to buy wine directly from the winery, which would cut their costs and make their supply chain more efficient by eliminating the distributor. Costco, in fact, has bankrolled two referendums in Washington state and sued it in federal court to liberalize the state's three-tier system. And the biggest producers, though not as vocal in their desire for change, would also like to eliminate three-tier so they could sell directly to the biggest retailers for the same reasons the biggest retailers want to buy directly.

Three-tier's biggest supporters are the distributors, some small and independent retailers, and the states. The retailers, who have seen service and pricing deteriorate in other industries as producers ignored them in favor of big customers, don't have to worry about that with three-tier. They may not get the pricing Costco gets, but it's not nearly as bad as what a local office supply store gets competing with Walmart. And the salesman or woman still makes regular calls. In addition, there are a variety of laws and regulations that make running their business easier, whether mandatory Sunday closing, price controls, or laws that prohibit grocery stores from selling wine and competing with them. The states have even more to lose. About a dozen, the so-called control states, sell liquor through some form of state store, which gives them a financial stake in three-tier's future. The rest see three-tier as the most effective way to regulate liquor (mostly for underage drinking and crime prevention), as well as the best way to collect taxes.

Quality wins out

Yet, somehow, quality cheap wine made it through this tangle of a mess of a system, in which what the consumer wants usually takes second place to what the wine business, aided and abetted by the Winestream Media, tells them they want. Nothing demonstrates the silliness of this system more than a study released in 2013 by a consultancy called Napa Technology, which said that the U.S.' "large Spanish-speaking population and the growing popularity of Spanish food seemed to be contributing to the growing popularity of Spanish varietals." It's as if Napa Technology didn't bother to do any research, given that Hispanics don't drink very much wine and that Spanish varietals aren't growing in popularity. These wines, made with grapes like tempranillo and albarino, are so insignificant in sales terms that the big national companies don't even bother to track them.

Quality cheap wine is on store shelves because the consumer, despite the difficulties built into the system, has sought it out. They have discovered the producers — hundreds, certainly, if not more — who have made the system work for them. They may be third-generation family operations like California's Bogle Vineyards, which has grown into a 1 million case company. They may be the century-old Domaine du Tariquet in southwest France in a region better known for cognac, or one of the handful of producers in Sicily who have reinvented the island's wine industry in favor of cost and value. They may even be an oddly-named subsidiary of a Big Wine company.

Even more telling? That these wine drinkers are the same people who aren't supposed to be drinking cheap wine. I once watched a woman with a pricey SUV in a Trader Joe's parking lot in Santa Fe. N.M., load cases of Two-buck Chuck into the car's tailgate. How odd, I thought, and chalked it up to something that could only happen in Santa Fe. But it wasn't odd — it was an insight into how the wine business really works, and not how we're supposed to think it works. That's because, says the Wine Market Council, 20 percent of the population buys 80 percent of the wine. The same people who are supposed to be fawning over scores and winespeak are voting with their dollars, and those dollars are being spent on the cheap wine that they're not supposed to like.

The next step, then, is twofold: First, for those who of us are part of the 20 percent to improve our skills and to better understand how to find the wines we like at a fair price, and the system be damned. Second, to help those who are not yet in that 20 percent to join us — to make wine education more relevant; to teach the newcomers the ins and outs of the three-tier system so they can use it to their advantage; and to help them understand why we appreciate wine and why we want to share our enthusiasm and our passion for it. And if our passion is cheap, well-made, high-value wine, so much the better.

The other thing to know is that those of most of the people who are in the 20 percent did not get there by magic. They were not born to wine, did not inherit a skill and a palate for it the way the British nobility inherit their land and their horses and their accents. Much of the 20 percent are Baby Boomers, who were the first U.S. generation to give wine a chance. There are many reasons for this, but mostly it was happenstance — a trip to Europe in college, a jug of wine shared between friends at a party. And the Boomers, as in so much else they did, created a demand for something where there had been no demand before.

In the process, they made a lot of people who sold wine and made wine and distributed wine and wrote about wine rich and famous. Not that those people helped the Boomers much — mostly, the Boomers did it on they own, and if they really learned something other than how to spend a lot of money to buy over-priced wine, it wasn't from scores but from a desire to learn and the idea that there may be something more to wine. How many Boomers came back from Europe with a completely different approach to wine? They saw first-hand that wine wasn't something to drink three or four times a year, but something that was a part of life in a way that Americans think other things are a part of life, be it baseball or working on cars or gardening. There was a joy and a pleasure to making wine a part of life, and it tasted good. What more could anyone want?

And if the Boomers, who didn't have the advantages that wine drinkers today have — instant reviews and information via the Internet, more and better wine available in more places and at better prices — could do this, why not the next two generations? Why isn't it possible for the young and the Hispanic and everyone else who feels excluded by wine, who sees it as elitist and confusing, who isn't sure what the fuss is about, whose families thought wine wasn't part of their culture, to become part of the 20 percent? Or, better yet, to increase that number to 25 or even 30 percent?

It should not only be possible — it should be a given. All they need is a chance. Let's give it to them.

Chapter II

The revolution in cheap wine

The free market may not work in many fields, but wine is a textbook case of how it operates to the benefit of consumers. . . . The first decade of the new century turned into a wonderful time for wine consumers, and that trend is likely to continue.

—George Taber, *A Toast to Bargain Wines*

The wine was called Avia. In the early 1980s, it cost $7 for three bottles at a grocery store in south Louisiana. It was made in the former Yugoslavia by the state-owned wine company, and its goal seemed to be two-fold: To provide the proletariat with cheap booze so they would be able to put up with living in a Communist country at the end of Communism, and to bring in desperately needed foreign exchange to help Yugoslavia weather the end of Communism. Regardless, it certainly wasn't made to taste like wine as we know wine today. There was very little varietal character; the chardonnay didn't taste particularly like chardonnay, the merlot didn't taste much like merlot, and so forth. The wines were rough and unpleasant, with harsh tannins and unripe fruit that gave the whites a greenish, crab apple flavor and the reds a bitter, acidic taste.

But I didn't know any better. It was wine, it was cheap, and it was available. So I drank it, and considered myself pretty sophisticated. After all, it was wine, and everyone else I knew was drinking Budweiser. The irony is that Avia was not an exception in those long ago days before Robert Parker, Kendall-Jackson chardonnay, and all the cute labels that clutter today's store shelves. Too much of the wine Americans drank, imported or otherwise, was of indifferent quality. Jug wine dominated the domestic market, and best thing most wine writers of the period had to say was that it was of low quality. And it's not like there were a lot of wine writers, either. Fewer than two dozen wrote regularly, mostly for magazines and all but a handful living in California.

And that's not all:

- The most important wine producing region in California was the Central Valley, which stretches 450 miles in the middle of the state and is nowhere near Napa and Sonoma in much of anything except geography.
- There were only 330 wineries in the entire state in 1975; today, there are almost twice that many in just Napa and Sonoma.
- The most important red wine grape was carignan, used to make red blends. Don't worry if you've never heard of it; few people knew what it was it was then, either. Neither cabernet sauvignon or merlot, the red grapes that are the basis for modern California wine as well as for the oceans of $10 grocery store wine we see every day, were widely planted.
- The most important white wine grape was colombard; its claim to fame then and today is that it is used to make brandy in France. The most popular white wine was made with colombard and chenin blanc and called chablis, and no one seemed to notice or care that it bore no relation to the

What the wine label tells you

PRODUCER → SMITH WINERY

VINTAGE
(YEAR GRAPES WERE
HARVESTED) → 2006

APPELLATION → California

→ Cabernet sauvignon

**VARIETAL
DESIGNATION**
OR NAME OF WINE

Produced and Bottled by Smith Winery, City, State

**ALCOHOL
CONTENT** → 12.5% ALC./VOL.   750 ML

GOVERNMENT WARNING: (I) ACCORDING TO THE SURGEON GENERAL, WOMEN SHOULD NOT DRINK ALCOHOLIC BEVERAGES DURING PREGNANCY BECAUSE F THE RISK OF BIRTH DEFECTS. (2) CONSUMPTION OF ALCOHOLIC BEVERAGES IMPAIRS YOUR ABILITY TO DRIVE A CAR OR OPERATE MACHINERY, AND MAY CAUSE HEALTH PROBLEMS.

CONTAINS SULFITIES

*Information
courtesy of Alcohol
and tobacco tax
and trade bureau*

white wine made with chardonnay in the Chablis region of Burgundy in France. Not that many growers planted char-donnay in California, either.

And, as Avia, demonstrated, imported wine was just as dicey. Yes, Europe made great wine — the Bordeauxs and Burgundies of France, the Riojas of Spain, and the high-end reds of Italy. But most wine drinkers couldn't afford them, even if they could find them. And they couldn't. There were no Costcos with pallets of wine stacked to the ceiling, no Whole Foods or Trader Joe's, and few liquor stores with more than a couple of locations. Most grocery stores probably carried more cooking wine than drinking wine, and what they did carry was heavy on sweet and Kosher; dessert wines were the best-selling wine category in the U.S. until 1967. If I wanted to trade up to a more expensive and theoretically better wine, it meant buying something like Barton & Guestier, a French label that cost $5 or $6 a bottle. It wasn't as offensive as the Avia, though its not-so-affectionate nickname — Barf & Gag — says most of what needs to be said about how it tasted. It should come as no surprise that wine geeks in the late 1970s and early 1980s drank Beaujolais, the French red that has been criti-cized over the past decade for being too simple and too fruity. In the early 1980s, though, that was high praise for a wine.

A long time ago

Today, that sounds like a story told by someone who grew up in a time before electricity and when people gave oranges for Christ-mas presents because they were such a novelty. None other than Jancis Robinson, one or the two or three pre-eminent wine critics in the world, has written: "The irony is that just as the difference in price between best and worst wines is greater than it has ever been, the difference in quality is narrower than ever before."

Wines like Avia, which used to be the rule, are the exception.

Walk into any store in the country, even a gas station that sells wine, and almost every bottle on the shelf will be clean, professionally made, and free of the flaws that were once so common — the unripe fruit, the moldy smells, the funky flavors, the battery acid finishes, the mouth-choking tannins, and the careless winemaking that made all of that possible. We can argue whether some cheap wines are too soft or too smooth or too fruity or if modern winemaking techniques have gone too far in the other direction, but we can't argue about whether today's cheap wines are drinkable. Because they are, and that they are has been revolutionary.

Yet, as revolutionary as it was, it's easy to figure out how it happened — improved winemaking technology, better viticultural practices, the enormous influence of the winemaking programs at colleges and universities in California and elsewhere, and the rise of the multi-national producers and the globalization of wine. Each is worthy of discussion, and particularly the last two.

What's not easy to figure out is why these things happened, because all of that quality appeared without any apparent reason. It's not as if, one day, the wine industry in all of its various forms rose up and said, "Never again!" By now, you should know wine doesn't work that way. One young winemaker, who has worked for both family-owned and multi-national producers, told me: "It's not that the revolution happened. It's that it took so long to happen. Should have happened years earlier."

The three-tier system, for one, actually works against improvement in quality. It doesn't give producers an incentive to make better wine because there's no guarantee there will be a market for it, and especially if it's a more expensive wine. Which, in the late 1970s and early 1980s, meant anything that cost more than jug wine, a couple of dollars a bottle. And the industry's traditional, constitutionally-protected, short-term mindset — "We're already making money, so why change?" doesn't exactly help either. Even today, after the revolution, too many producers still chase customers instead of quality, making wine they think consumers will buy instead of the best, most honest wine they can, and not understanding that the best, most honest wine can also be profitable. This is part of a larger metaphysical dilemma that haunts American business, and that affects quality in so many other industries: Profit itself isn't enough — we have to have more, always more. So too many wine companies focus on short-term profits and not long-term viability. These producers don't ask, "Is the wine any good?" Instead, it's "What score will it get?" Or, "Have we got that flavor profile right for that target demographic?"

The best explanation about what happened? That the advances in technology and education and the rise of the multi-nationals forced the industry to slowly change, even if it didn't see a need to change. New people, new ideas, and new approaches made a difference, and you can see this difference in the improved quality and lower prices in the 25-year period leading up to the beginning of the 21st century. The catch is that it's not easy to trace this change, because almost everyone has a different perspective. Ask a grape grower, and they'll talk about how they gave the wineries better fruit, and so the wineries were forced to make better wine whether they wanted to or not. Ask the universities, and they'll talk about how they provided the industry with better-educated winemakers and growers, who used what they learned to make better wine. Ask the wineries, and they'll talk about their more consumer-oriented approach to winemaking — easier to drink wines that offered better value. There's even a school of thought that credits consumers, who were fed up with the wines they were drinking in the late 1970s and early 1980s and demanded better quality. There may even be some truth to this, given that per capita wine consumption in the U.S. peaked in 1985 and didn't return to that level until the mid-2000s.

How cheap wine quality got better in the 21st century

• Grape growing and winemaking degree programs at UC-Davis and Fresno State

• Big Wine, and the growth of multi-national producers

• Better viticultural practices to improve the quality of grapes

• New winemaking technology made it easier to make quality wine

In this, the one constant was generational change, the wine industry's equivalent of the Hebrews' 40 years in the desert. The men (because they were almost all men) who had led the industry out of Prohibition retired or died, and gave way to younger men (because they were almost all men) who were better educated, more aware of modern grape growing and winemaking techniques, and understood the importance of the consumer in a way the older generation didn't. Think of it as the difference between someone who grew up with dial telephones and someone who grew up with smart phones. The former knows what a smart phone is and can use it, but never quite understands it or appreciates it in a way the person who grew up with the smart phone does. The latter will use the camera at almost any opportunity, for example, while the former may not even know the phone has a camera. One of the best examples of this change in generational mindset was the switch to what the industry called "fighting varietals" in the mid-1980s. That's when the younger generation abandoned the reliance on jug wines, chablis, and red blends made with carignan in favor of wines made with one kind of grape, including cabernet, merlot, and chardonnay and that cost $3 to $5 a bottle — the precursor to today's $10 wine.

The catalyst for the fighting varietals was chardonnay, and Glen Ellen and Sutter Home were perhaps the two wineries that did the best job of bringing chardonnay and the fighting varietals to the U.S. consumer (as well as white zinfandel, which was accidentally invented at Sutter Home in 1972). Their wines were clean, fruity, well-priced and widely available — something that, as noted, was not necessarily true before then. When I switched from Avia to Glen Ellen in the mid-1980s, the difference was stunning. It's no coincidence, either, that Glen Ellen's managing general partner was in his mid-30s back then, and that the brand sold 1.5 million cases in 1987 — compared to 6,450 in 1982. Wrote Fortune magazine in 1988: "America's taste in wine, never especially elevated, is ratcheting up, and that means a shakeout ahead for California vintners."

Getting better and better

Which brings the discussion back to the whys, which start with better winemaking and better viticultural (what happens in the vineyard) practices. Both improved so much that it's difficult to believe that the change could have happened in such a short period of time, since 30 years in the context of the 2,500-year history of wine is no time at all. But it did, with a host of technical and practical improvements that were as simple as better hygiene and cleaner wineries to things that are too complex to go into, like the role of fluid dynamics in the fermentation process and the development of new grape varieties and clones of existing varieties.

The center of all that change was education, a particularly American approach to any problem. It's not too much of a simplification to say that whenever we want to improve how we do something, we set up a degree program. West Point, the U.S. military academy, is one of the oldest in the world, and the U.S. is far from the oldest country, while Horace Mann, who developed the modern system of universal public education, did it in New England in the first half of the 19th century.

Hence the crucial — and still, perhaps, not appreciated as much as they should be — roles that the University of California at Davis and Fresno State University have played in improving wine quality. Says wine critic Robert Whitley: "Davis and Fresno have played a huge role in quality improvement, and the difference in California wine today, and around the world, is the absence of flaws at all price levels. Even cheap wines taste good. They may not have the heft or structure of the expensive wines, but they are pleasant and satisfying for the vast legions of wine-drinking families that can't afford to put a $30 wine on the dinner table every night."

College programs in agriculture are not new, and the Midwest and South have had universities with programs to teach corn, wheat, and cotton farmers how to be better corn, wheat and cotton farmers for decades — and no one thinks much about it. What's different here is that the programs are for wine — something that was illegal for part of the 20th century and not especially popular for much of the time after that, even in California. This points to something that most wine drinkers aren't necessarily aware of — the tremendous economic impact that wine plays in the California economy. It accounts for one-third of a million jobs in the state, almost two percent of the state's total employment. Some 21 million tourists spend what the Wine Institute trade group estimates to be $2.1 billion each year. Those aren't corn or cotton numbers, but they'll do.

Which makes the student-run winery at Fresno more than just another after-school activity. Or that the curriculum at the two schools reflects that serious economic impact. Wine may be revered in poetry and verse, and rarely does anyone in the Winestream Media consider the practical aspects, but in practice it's just like corn, cotton, and soybeans. The classes for graduate and undergraduate students at Davis and Fresno are scientific, technical and practical — subjects like organic chemistry, agricultural economics, wine microbiology, and food science. Not a lot of romance in those, is there?

Or, as the 133-year-old wine program at Davis explains itself:

Our instructional programs in Viticulture and Enology are designed to teach students the scientific principles that underlie growing grapes and making wine, and the basic skills needed to apply these principles. Our program is not designed to teach a particular style of winemaking,

winery management, grape cultivation or vineyard management. However, based on their detailed understanding of the process, graduates are expected to develop their
own style with some tutelage and experience. Students
are advised to seek out additional business management
skills if they expect to manage a business. In some cases,
this can be incorporated into the B.S. degree program.

In this, the schools are not the only top-notch viticulture and
enology programs in the U.S., and anyone reading this who went
to one of the others is probably already composing an angry
e-mail. It's also worth noting the efforts at the University of Bordeaux, where important research has gone on since the 1880s.
Though, and this underscores the more important role that education has played in the U.S., Bordeaux didn't offer a winemaking
degree until 1956 and its programs didn't become a full-fledged
part of the university until 1971.

The point is that Davis, which helped the California industry
recover from Prohibition, and Fresno, which first offered classes
in the 1950s and where the degree program is about a decade old,
are the examples that the newest schools use when they set up
their programs. It's probably not surprising that Davis and Fresno
are fierce rivals, as competitive as any two sports teams, and that
sometimes it's not necessarily a friendly rivalry.

Still, the work each has done speaks for itself:

- Davis officials estimate that more than 95 percent of the
  grapes grown in the U.S., as well as many around the world,
  came from plants that originated at the school.
- Davis researchers in the 1950s did pioneering work in dis-
  covering the relationship between bacteria and wine quality
  and why wine spoiled.
- Fresno's student-run winery was built in 1997, making it the
  first college in the country with a bonded winery on campus.

- Fresno has been a leader to better figure out the relationship between wine grapes and tannins, something that
  has bedeviled winemakers working with red wine for
  generations.

Making progress

This idea of education to improve winemaking is relatively
new — really in the past 50 years or so, not a very long period
given the 500-year history of the modern wine business. Before
the last half of the 20th century, wine education was rarely formal;
rather, it was handed down and passed along from winemaker to
winemaker, from family to family, from region to region. This is
perfectly understandable, because all wine was local before the
middle of the 20th century. Spaniards rarely drank French wine,
and Spaniards in Rioja in northern Spain rarely drank wine
from anywhere else in Spain. The same logic held true through-
out Europe. Why would anyone in Bordeaux want to drink Burgundy? They had plenty of Bordeaux, didn't they?

Some of this attitude was parochial, but much of it was a function of Europe's primitive, pre-modern supply chain. Supply chain
is the fancy, though very accurate, term that details the path that
raw materials take to become finished products, and wine has
never been very supply chain friendly. It's difficult and expensive
to make and bulky and expensive to transport, even today. Hence,
in those long ago days before rail, it made little economic sense
to sell wine to another region. Port, which was heavily exported,
is the exception that proves this rule. Ordinary table wine would
have spoiled during long, hot sea voyages before steam power or
refrigeration, so Portuguese winemakers fortified their wines
with spirits, which acted as a preservative.

So, given the local nature of wine, why should someone in
France want to learn what was going on in Spain or what kind of

grape growing or wine making problems the Spanish were having? Or, even, in another part of France? They used different grapes and the weather and soil were different. Nothing happening elsewhere could make any difference, could it? The fallacy in this approach was more than amply demonstrated in the late 19th and early 20th centuries, when the phylloxera louse nearly destroyed the French wine industry and devastated much of the rest of Europe. The bug, which burrows into the grape's roots, hampers the vine's ability to take in water and nutrients and usually kills it. In this, it infests grapevines regardless of region, and Bordeaux winemakers were forced to collaborate with their Burgundy and Rhone colleagues (to say nothing of working with winemakers in Germany, Spain, and Italy) to combat the louse.

In other words, education combined with research. The solution they found for phylloxera is still used today, since the bug is remarkably resistant to chemicals. American researchers, including a Texan named T.V. Munson, discovered that the bug didn't infest native American rootstocks. The next step, then, was for Europeans and Americans to find a resistant rootstock that could be grafted to European grapevines without affecting the quality of the fruit (in much the same way gardeners graft roses to produce better flowers and new colors). This was a painstaking process, and took years to complete.

This is just one example of how primitive much of wine was before (and even after) the Industrial Revolution. Commercial yeasts, for one, were a fantasy, and the yeast that started fermentation in pre-19th century wine was naturally occurring, and hence a mystery to winemakers. Fermentation is easy to control with commercial yeast, and the winemaker knows exactly when and how to start and stop the process. With natural yeast, though, much of that is guesswork combined with experience, making it that much more difficult to control the quality of the wine. Yet, in those pre-collaboration days, if someone in remote southern Italy had figured out how to use yeast more effectively, there's no guarantee anyone else would have learned about it, and winemakers would have continued to stumble around trying to figure out why their fermentation failed.

Formal education, starting in Bordeaux (a botany professor named Pierre-Marie-Alexis Millarde played a key role in the phylloxera fight) and evolving into the American-style system pioneered at Davis and used almost everywhere in the world today, was the answer. Research, under the auspices of a wine education program, would solve problems, and then the solution would be passed to winemakers in a systematic and orderly fashion (which is how the great American agricultural colleges have also functioned). In fact, this is mostly what happened with yeast. French researchers at Bordeaux, following up on Louis Pasteur's work (he not only invented pasteurization, but did important work with yeast), found a way to add yeast to wine in a more controlled process. This improved quality and reduced spoilage.

The second important development in improving wine quality is even newer — barely as old as the 21st century. That's the arrival of Big Wine — the multi-national producers that in about a decade have come to dominate production and sales of most of the wine that we drink. The Winestream Media and the wine snobs dismiss Big Wine because its wines are boring, corporate and cheap, and unworthy of its attention. Eric Asimov of the New York Times, who may be the best wine writer in the world, once famously said he didn't care if anyone drank YellowTail, the $7 Australian brand that is the third biggest seller in the U.S, because that wasn't his audience. And if Asimov is the best, can you imagine what the rest of his colleagues think?

This is like ignoring Walmart because it's corporate, its stores are boring, and too many people shop there.

BIG WINE

U.S. wine sales by company

22.8% E & J Gallo Winery

15.9% The Wine Group

12.8% Constellation Brands

4.9% Trinchero Family Estates

4.5% Treasury Wine Estates

3.5% Bronco Wine Co.

35.6% Everyone else

Information from
Michigan State study, 2013

In fact, it's almost impossible to underestimate the impact Big Wine has made on the U.S. and the world. Just six companies account for almost 65 percent of wine sales in the U.S., and they have more than 200 brands between them. These six — E&J Gallo, The Wine Group, Constellation Brands. Treasury Wine Estates, and Trinchero Family Estates, and Bronco Wine — are so big that YellowTail, despite the 8 million cases it sells, is only the seventh largest wine company in the U.S.

Getting bigger and bigger

This immenseness is staggering. The three biggest producers sell more than one-half the wine sold in the U.S.; this figure surprised even Michigan State's Phil Howard, who studies consolidation in the U.S. beverage business and compiled the numbers. "Wine was much different than what I thought," he said. "If you go to the stores, it seems like you have all these choices, because the shared ownership is not very apparent." And Big Wine is going to get even bigger. Howard estimates that wine is about where beer was in the 1950s, when 30 companies dominated the U.S. beer market. Today, just two beer producers — AB InBev and Molson Coors — account for three-quarters of all sales.

Howard's research spotlights the importance of cheap wine in all of this. The backbone of wine sales in the U.S. are wines that even those of us who pay attention to cheap wine don't usually notice (let alone the Winestream Media). The Carlo Rossi jug wines were Gallo's biggest seller in 2011 in terms of volume, even bigger than its high-flying Barefoot brand. Cook's champagne, which costs about $5 and is owned by Constellation, is about as important in terms of market share as the much better known and even Winestream Media-reviewed Robert Mondavi. The biggest wine companies have become bigger and gained more market share, buying out well-established independents in the process, much as happened in beer since the 1950s. About one-third of the producers in the first WineBusiness.com listing of the country's 30 largest wineries in 2003 are gone, either sold or merged into another company. And big is often not big enough; witness Constellation's purchase of Mark West in 2012, in which the Mark West boss said his 600,000 case winery was too small to compete in the modern marketplace — and, with those 600,000 cases, Mark West was the 20th biggest producer in the U.S. that year.

In this, Big Wine understands the wine business' dirty little secret better than anyone else — the vast majority of consumers buy on price. They don't care about scores or appellation or even the grape used to make the wine. Give them something that tastes good, which usually means fruity or sweet or both, and that isn't overpriced, and they're happy. Or, as a friend of mine who is as typical a U.S. wine drinker as they get always says when we talk about wine and I wax too poetic: "It's just a beverage."

This is a difference that Big Wine has leveraged to its advantage. Wineries, traditionally small, family businesses, have traditionally had all the problems of small, family businesses — not enough capital; not enough employees, and especially talented ones; indifferent management skills; and the inability to successfully market their product, mostly because they don't see the need and couldn't afford to do marketing even if they did. Capital is especially important, since wine is equipment intensive — barrels, tanks, fermenters, and even temperature-controlled warehouses. Making the least expensive white wine requires a stainless steel tank that costs $1,000, and even a small winery may need a dozen tanks. Compounding these problems is the three-tier system, which favors large producers over small because the former can more easily and more cheaply provide more product for sale. Distributors hate running out of of something, and that happens all the time with smaller wineries.

Big Wine has none of those problems. Its companies have access to the world's financial markets just like any other multi-national (and, like other multi-nationals, preferential treatment when it comes to borrowing money, selling bonds, and so forth). It can take advantage of massive economies of scale, whether in buying bottles or wine barrels. This economic clout has helped them revolutionize the wine supply chain, allowing them to use grapes from anywhere in the world for their grocery store wines and to pay less in the process, which in turn helps lower the price of their wine and makes it more appealing to the biggest retailers, the Costcos and Walmarts, which sell mostly on price. And Big Wine has no trouble attracting talented employees — its companies were the first to hire women in responsible positions in a business that had traditionally been male from the vineyards to the wine room to the front office.

Big Wine also understands marketing in a way that all but a few small producers do. They're so good at marketing — as good, in some ways, as consumer products giants like McDonald's and Procter & Gamble — that it almost doesn't matter what's in the bottle. Does anyone buy Cupcake, owned by The Wine Group, because it's "quality wine" in the way wine writers think of wine? Of course not. They buy it because it has a cute name and fun label and clever writing and because it tastes smooth and fruity and maybe even a little sweet. Calling a Cupcake wine Red Velvet is close to genius. Smaller producers don't know how to perform this kind of marketing sleight of hand; even if they did, they probably wouldn't have the money to market it effectively.

Big Wine not only improved the quality of the product but the consumer's perception of it. It hired the graduates of the wine programs and took advantage of the research being done at Davis, Fresno, and elsewhere, as well as the changes in technology and grape growing to make wine taste consistently the same. This consistency, given the vagaries of winemaking and grape growing, which include but aren't limited to weather, had been almost impossible to achieve for much of the past 500 years. Hence the need for vintage charts, which graded the quality of wine made with grapes harvested in a certain year. They seem almost quaint in the post-modern era, when winemakers can use high-tech yeasts, advanced blending techniques, and who knows what else to make this vintage taste like the last one, as well as the one before that and even the one before that one.

Bring on the fruit

Big Wine focuses on making fruity, almost sweet wines aimed at a U.S. consumer who has been raised on sweetness, whether soft drinks or the hundreds of food items flavored with high fructose corn syrup that are part of the American diet — canned soup, ketchup, breakfast cereal, and the like. In this, the wines are not poorly made or flawed — again, Big Wine understands quality control — as much as they don't taste the way they have traditionally tasted. For hundreds of years, pinot noir tasted a certain way — dark, almost earthy, with little fruit. Over the past decade, Big Wine, with products like Mark West, made wine it called pinot noir but that tasted completely different — fruity and yes, smooth, the descriptor that consumers always use and that always makes the Winestream Media's hair stand on end. That Big Wine's pinot noir didn't taste like traditional pinot nor (and that it sold for as little as $10 a bottle) bothered only those same wine writers.

The irony is that Big Wine, before this century, had failed miserably to do anything close to what it has done in the past 15 years. The wine business was supposed to be conglomerate-proof, and there was example after example to prove the point. Coca-Cola went into the California wine business in 1977, but its effort lasted just five years. It sold its holdings to Seagram's — at the time a huge multi-national drinks company — but Seagram's then sold most of its wine business in the late 1980s and was completely out of it by 2000. The difference between those failures and what has happened since is that today's Big Wine understands the business in a way companies like Coke and Seagram's never did.

Constellation, for example, was once tiny Canandaigua, an upstate New York winery that made Richard's Wild Irish Rose and Kosher wines. But the Sands family, which started the company, still runs it. And the Sands, despite Constellation's publicly-traded size and billions of dollars in sales, recognize, like the Gallo family that still controls the privately-held E&J Gallo, that winemaking is as much farming as anything else. This was an alien concept to Coke, whose products are made with water and high fructose corn syrup, and to Seagram's, which also had holdings in chemicals and movies in the 1980s and 1990s. Wine, to them, was just a product extension, and, in that, their approach was not that much different from Avia's — making the cheapest possible product for all the wrong reasons.

Cheap wine has come a long way since then.

Chapter III

Understanding cheap wine

A glass of the old cooking wine.
> —Horace Rumpole, *Rumpole of the Bailey*

Horace Rumpole, the fictional barrister created by novelist John Mortimer, understood the value of cheap wine. Every day after work, he could be found at Pommeroy's Wine Bar, rehashing his battles with cranky judges, nit-witted prosecutors, pretentious colleagues, and She Who Must Be Obeyed over a glass or three of Pommery's house wine, a red French blend also fondly referred to as Chateau Thames Embankment or Chateau Fleet Street (named after the bar's London location). As Rumpole noted more than once, the wine's great attribute was its price, which was so inexpensive that he could afford it even when waiting interminably for the government to pay him for defending his mostly indigent (and guilty) clients.

But this is not to say that Rumpole, because all he could afford was cheap wine, was intimidated by those who assumed they were his betters, be they wine connoisseurs or Queen's Counsels. Mortimer, a wine drinker who drank a glass of Champagne every morning in his retirement (but "not very grand Champagne"), wrote a story called "Rumpole and the Blind Tasting." Rumpole's knowledge of cheap wine helped him solve a wine fraud involving crooked retailers, wine snobs, an overwhelmed member of the Winestream Media, and a fellow barrister, the insufferable Claude Erskine-Brown (who had dared to criticize Rumpole's taste in wine). The key to the mystery? That Rumpole figured something was up because the expensive wine that everyone said was wonderful didn't taste much better than his Chateau Thames Embankment.

Which makes Rumpole the kind of wine drinker we need more of. Experience and an open mind are more important than all of the scores and Winestream Media articles in the world. It's about tasting wine, remembering what you tasted, and then tasting more wine. Drink what you like, but be willing to try things you may not like. The process is not complicated, it doesn't require a graduate degree or deep pockets, and it's OK if you can't tell boysenberry fruit from tobacco and leather. Learning about wine requires answering nothing more than The Two Questions: Did you like the wine? Why did you like it? The rest is *lagniappe* — fun and enjoyable, certainly, but not altogether necessary to understanding wine.

The problem that most Americans face is that they're taught just the opposite — and they believe it. This attitude, given the skepticism of our age, has always been difficult to understand. Lots of people believe the U.S. didn't send an astronaut to the moon or that there are vast conspiracies at work in the federal government, but they accept as gospel that they should only drink certain kinds of wine, that old, mostly white men are the only people qualified to tell them what wine to drink, and that they should drink the wine that the old, mostly white men tell them to. Or else.

That's because those old, mostly white men have something

called a palate, which no one else does. Technically, palate has two meanings. First, wine tasting as a physical process, which the ultimately authoritative "Oxford Companion to Wine" describes as "the combined human tasting faculties in the mouth, and, sometimes nose." Second, the ability to taste wine, as in "she has a good palate" just like "she is a good basketball player." Both matter when learning about wine, because both help answer The Two Questions.

Not all palates, as defined by the second meaning, are created equal. Some of us are better at tasting wine than others, though the difference is not what most of us assume it to be. A Yale scientist, Linda Bartoshuk, divides the world into three groups: Super tasters, about 25 percent of the population; tasters, about 50 percent; and non-tasters, about 25 percent. The first group is above average, the second is average, and the third is below average. Women are a little more than twice as likely to be super tasters as men, according to Bartoshuk's research, and I can attest to that from my experience. Women have some of the best palates I know, much better than mine.

The problem with these studies is not the science, but how they are interpreted. A 2012 study, conducted by researchers at Penn State and Brock University in Canada, found that the so-called experts can taste subtleties in wine that the rest of us can't. This was not earth-shattering news, tying in as it does to Bartoshuk's work, as well as variety of other studies over the past decade (including a 2001 effort at the University of Bordeaux, in which oenology students couldn't tell red wine from white). There is little doubt that some of us taste wine better than others, just as some of us jump higher or dance with more skill. But the 2012 study was immediately trumpeted by the Winestream Media as evidence of its superiority, and as one more reason why we should drink what they tell us to drink. But it was used even by non-wine media outlets like National Public Radio and the Huffington Post to reinforce the assumption that the so-called experts are all super-tasters, and that if you aren't a super taster, you can't possibly enjoy wine.

The big lie

Which is obviously, patently, not true. Do people who don't understand the internal combustion engine have difficulty driving a car? I was quite possibly the worst softball player in the world. I couldn't throw, my swing was slow and powerless, and I ran like a cardboard box. But I loved playing softball, whether it was in gym class or recreational leagues. Yet, by applying the logic of wine, I should not have enjoyed softball, and should never have played it. The flaw with this reasoning, as Washington Post wine columnist Dave McIntyre has pointed out, is that almost every wine drinker who isn't an expert doesn't spend as much time with wine as the experts do. "If as a wine writer I'm an 'expert,' it's because I've taken the time and made the effort to taste more wines than most people have," he wrote. "Taste enough cabernet sauvignon and you'll learn to tell it from merlot, if you pay attention. . . . The key words there are 'if you pay attention.'"

The typical consumer, based on U.S. wine consumption statistics, drinks less than two or three dozen bottles of wine a year. A competent wine writer, retailer, restaurateur, or sommelier will taste almost 1,000, and some even two or three times that many. That's the difference, and it doesn't have anything to do with the quality of your palate. Experience is all, and not some super mystical wine chakra that the experts are supposed to have and that no one else does. But ordinary wine drinkers are so confused and befuddled by the process that they don't know that this difference exists. They only know what they've been told, and that's that it must be their fault that they can't tell boysenberry from toasty and oaky. Obviously, they must be flawed in some way.

The other difference? The experts, as McIntyre notes, pay attention (or least the good ones do). That means tasting the wine carefully — sipping as opposed to gulping, noting its flavors and attributes, and thinking about what he or she tasted. Then, they record it: The name of the wine, the cost, what their impressions were, and whether they would recommend it to someone else. This is hardly rocket science, says McIntyre: "People often tell me, 'I had a great wine the other night!' When I ask what wine, they hem and haw and say, 'Umm, it had a green label.' I can't help those people. Even if someone wants to spend only $5 to $10 on a bottle, paying attention helps distinguish the [junk] from the gems — and yes, there are gems in that price range."

Recording what you've tasted is as simple as taking a picture of the label with your phone and making a note about the price and whether you liked it or not. Don't worry if your prose doesn't read like something from "The Wine Snob's Guide to Beauty and Wonderfulness;" all you're trying to do is remind yourself, later, whether you want to buy the wine again. Or, even better, try something similar, neither of which should be revolutionary concepts. Specifically, you'll want to record the wine, the price, where you bought it, what it tasted like, and whether you think it's worth the money.

The last two items are especially important. Winespeak has intimidated so many consumers that, as one once told me, the idea of describing what a wine tastes like seems as difficult as doing geometry proofs. How can someone possibly identify those obscure fruit flavors? The point is that you don't have to identify them. All you need to do is to describe the wine the way you tasted it, since you're the only one who matters. Robert Parker isn't going to grade your tasting notes.

Whether a wine is worth the money — whether it provides value — is as crucial. Too often, the experts see price as insignificant in the consumer decision to buy a wine. Not enough wine writers, retailers, sommeliers, and restaurateurs buy the wine they drink. It's given to them by the producer or distributor, and the only worry the last three have about price is whether they can sell the wine for what it costs (which is much different from whether it's worth what it costs). Too many writers, meanwhile, see price as a function of hipness — the more expensive the wine, the cooler it is to write about and the more famous they'll become for writing about it. This is one reason why so few writers bother with cheap wine.

There are a variety of ways to track your wine drinking — an old-fashioned notebook; a spreadsheet with columns for price, date, wine and tasting notes, and the like; and free software and apps like CellarTracker (which I use), and most of which work on traditional computers or phones or both. This process is not complicated; the most difficult thing about doing it is keeping up. Once you fall a couple of bottles behind, it's like to trying to clean the garage. No matter how good your intentions, it never seems to get done. Still, once you've compiled a 12- or 15-month wine drinking history, and you'll be able to do this even if you only drink those two or three dozen bottle of wine a year, you'll be able to talk about wine the way the experts do (though, hopefully, with less arrogance).

Knowing the basics

But, say the skeptics, it can't be this easy. You must be leaving something out. But not really — that process will get almost any wine drinker to the McIntyre Point, so that they will be able to distinguish plonk from gems. Along the way, there are things that are helpful to understand:

- A wine's color comes from its skin, not the grape itself. Peel a grape, and all are the same, sort of clear-ish. When red

Three things everyone should know about wine

- Think well-made wine and poorly-made wine instead of good and bad

- A wine's color comes from its skin, not the grape itself

- Tannins cause the astringent, unpleasant flavor that is one of the reasons why so many people say they don't like red wine

wine is made, the skins are left in the fermenting grape juice and their color bleeds into the juice. The skins aren't usually left on when fermenting white wine, so white wine is clear. Rose and pink wines are usually made with red grapes, and the skins are left in contact with the grape juice long enough to produce the desired color, whether light pink (less contact time) or darker (more time).

- Think well-made wine and poorly-made wine instead of good and bad. Good and bad are relative; what one person thinks is good — dry, rough, and with very little fruit — could be someone else's idea of wine that needs to be poured down the sink. A well-made wine, regardless of anything else, is balanced. The alcohol, fruitiness, sweetness, and acidity play off each other, and one doesn't dominate the others. A cheap wine can be balanced; an expensive can be woefully out of whack.

- Vintage is the year the grapes used to make the wine were harvested, so a wine label that says 2013 means that the grapes in the wine were picked in 2013. But vintage doesn't matter for 90 percent of the world's wine and the idea of good years and bad years is fast becoming a wine geek fiction. Winemakers are skilled enough and have so much technology available that they can work around most harvest-related flaws for all but the most expensive wine. Where vintage does matter is for cheap wine and shelf life. Older, less expensive wines can wear out, turn to vinegar, or oxidize if they're too old — generally, that limit is two years for a white and three for a red.

- A well-made wine should have three flavors — in the front of the mouth, in the middle, and in the back. This is something that wine geeks often go into spasms of joy discussing. If you want to watch someone's eyes grow wide and their face flush, ask about taste receptors in the mouth and their relationship to umami. It's enough to know, with enough experience, that you'll be able to notice whether there is a flavor in the front, middle and back.

- Tannins, next to fruit, are the most noticeable flavor in wine. Technically, they aren't a flavor, but a puckery feeling in the back of the mouth that is caused by tannic acid, but most wine drinkers identify them as such. Tannic acid comes mostly from the grape skins, seeds, and stems, and red wines have noticeably more tannins than white wines. That's because the skins aren't left in contact with the juice in white wines the way they are in red. The tannins are the stuff that causes the astringent, unpleasant flavor that is one of the reasons why so many people say they don't like red wine, though tannins don't have to be unpleasant and are actually a key part of well-made wine.

Wine flavors may well be the most confusing part of wine, and the bit that makes so many consumers run screaming for soft drinks, sweet tea, beer, and flavored vodka. Ask a typical wine drinker to describe a wine, and one of the first adjectives they'll use will be smooth. Ask someone in the Winestream Media or one of its disciples among wine drinkers to describe a wine, and one of the last adjectives they'll use will be smooth. Unctuous, maybe: a term that goes a long way towards explaining why consumers are so confused. Has anyone ever used unctuous to describe other kinds of fruit products?

Wine flavors occur naturally, and not from additions or flavorings unless the wine is specifically labeled that way — chocolate wine, peach wine, and so forth. Grapes are fruit, just like tomatoes, and have many of the same volatile compounds (including ethanol, glucose, and glycerol for the chemically inclined). Why tomatoes? Because they can vary in flavor the same way that

Three flavor explanation

Well-made wine should have three flavors —

in the front of the mouth, *in the middle,* *and in the back.*

grapes can. Or, as Scientific American has put it: "A tomato's flavor depends not only on the balance of sugars and acids within the fruit, but also on subtle aromatic compounds." Some tomatoes are sweet, others are acidic, some are more tomato-like than others, some are less, and so forth. It's easy to taste those differences in tomatoes, and no one has a second thought about it. But when an expert says a sauvignon blanc tastes like grapefruit, how many ordinary wine drinkers wonder how that's possible? How many think: "Did someone add grapefruit juice, and will people make fun of me if I ask that?"

But wine's flavors don't have to be confusing. White wine tastes of lighter fruit flavors, like apples, pears, peaches, and citrus. Red wine tastes of darker fruit flavors, like berries and cherries. More specifically, chardonnay tastes of apples and pears. Sauvignon blanc tastes of citrus. Moscato is often most definitely orange. Riesling can have a an almost mineral flavor. Merlot tastes of blueberries, while cabernet sauvignon is more cherry-like. Pinot noir can be almost mushroom-ish if it's from France, but raspberry or even strawberry if it's from California or Oregon.

Yet, having said all this, it's OK if you can't identify specific fruit flavors. The important thing is whether you can taste the difference between one wine and another. All wine does not taste the same, even though one of the goals of grocery store wine producers seems to be to dumb it down as much as possible, and especially to make all reds taste fruity and almost sweet — the soft drink formula that their focus groups tell them is the key to success with the U.S. wine consumer.

One place that doesn't help wine drinkers identify fruit flavors, or even much of what the wine tastes like, is the back label. The back label may well be the most dishonest and cynical part of the wine business, designed not to educate but to flimflam the wine drinker into buying something without actually telling them any-

Wine flavors

• White wine tastes of lighter fruit flavors, like apples, pears, peaches, and citrus. Red wine tastes of darker fruit flavors, like berries and cherries.

• Wine flavors occur naturally, and not from additions or flavorings unless the wine is specifically labeled that way.

• Oak aging gives wine a vanilla and often caramel flavor, more noticeable in white wines than red.

thing about the wine. Why else would a back label say things like "a handcrafted wine that has become a classic" for a label that has been in business for just five years? Or wax poetic about the "Fuji apple flavors" in a $6 wine, given that most of us have no idea what a Fuji apple tastes like — let alone how such a complex flavor could get into such a cheap wine.

There are two kinds of this back label (call it the back baloney, if you will). Typically, they're on grocery store wines that cost between $6 and $20 and usually have a cute front label. The first, like the label talking about classics above, doesn't describe the wine, but makes the wine buyer feel special for buying it. How about a wine made for someone who "prizes the simple things in life: spending good times with close friends"? This image marketing isn't new, and there are examples all around us. The difference is that they're in ads for $50,000 cars and not cheap bottles of wine. The second style uses descriptors to bedazzle, so that the poor consumer thinks the wine tastes like chocolate cake or cinnamon coffee or blueberry pie instead of what it really tastes like, which is wine made with grapes that have been manipulated so that the final product has enough fruit flavor so that it can be described as a baked good, soft drink, or something else suitably fruity and sweet. What's missing from the second kind of label, interestingly, are descriptors used for traditionally dry red wines, like mushrooms, cedar, and leather. Even wines that fit that profile sometimes play up fruity and sweet, which says a lot about the focus of the marketing approach.

The saddest part about all this is that the back label doesn't have to be so silly. The International Riesling Foundation has done ground-breaking work with its labels, developing a sensible, easy-to-decipher chart that tells consumers where that particular wine fits on a sliding scale from sweet to dry. Other wines, which more often than not seem to be made for retailers like Aldi whose customers are not sophisticated wine drinkers, have similar labels. They pinpoint the wine's fruitiness and sweetness on a sliding scale; the irony here is that these wines are produced as private labels by the same companies who espouse the virtues of Fuji apples. But more can—and should be—done. How about a recommended, industry-wide standard label, written in English and not winespeak, and based on the riesling foundation sliding scale, that offers information that consumers need. How dry is the wine? What temperature should it be served at? How fruity is it? What are possible pairings? What are its flavors, using words like rich and robust or more accurate fruit terms, like citrus or green apple?

The back label needs to be less confusing because it deals with one of the most important—and perplexing—differences in wine, between those that are fruity and those that are sweet. Many wine drinkers, who have been taught that sweet wine is evil and beneath them, are constantly on the lookout for sweet wine. Because, of course, they aren't supposed to drink it. So they will confuse wine that is fruity, like sauvignon blanc or vigonier, with wine that is sweet, like riesling, despite the significant differences between fruity and sweet.

A dry wine, very simply, is a wine that isn't sweet—nothing more complicated than that. Most of the wine sold in the U.S., save for white zinfandel, moscato, riesling, and some sweet red blends, is dry, and that holds true whether the wine is red, white, or pink. So why the confusion? Because most people associate dry wine with red wine, and with the puckery sensation in the mouth that tannins cause. If the puckery sensation is missing, then the wine must be sweet and they shouldn't drink it. Because, after all, wine needs to be manly. But tannins have very little to do with dryness. A wine can be tannic and sweet, like poorly-made port or some of the new sweet reds. And white wines, which usually don't have noticeable tannins, can be just as dry as red wines.

Make mine fruity

That's something many wine drinkers have difficulty understanding. Americans are so accustomed to equating fruitiness with sweetness, like in jams and jellies, that when they smell or taste a fruit flavor, they assume that it's sweet — even when it isn't. James Tidwell, a master sommelier, says the confusion comes from the difference in flavors we can taste vs. the aromas we can smell. We can taste four things — sweet, sour, salty, and bitter (as well as umami, which isn't so much a taste as a sensation, and doesn't exactly apply here). On the other hand, we can identify thousands of smells, though what's worth noting is that none of them can be identified as sweet. A baked apple, for instance, doesn't smell sweet, but fruity and of cinnamon and even of caramel. It's sweet when we taste it, though, from the sugar added to the apple, so what does our brain do? It equates the aromas with the baked apple's sweetness, so when we smell it the next time experience tells us that it smells sweet — even though it really doesn't.

The same thing holds true for wine. A typical $10 California merlot is just bursting with ripe, mouth-filling blueberry flavor. But the wine itself doesn't have enough sugar to be sweet, since the sugar in the grape juice was converted to alcohol during the winemaking process. Its fruitiness is a function of its volatile compounds. But when we smell the wine, our brain associates the blueberry aroma with sweetness, and we just know that the wine is sweet, even though there is actually no measurable sugar in it.

This contradiction drives consumers crazy, and is one reason why so many rely on tannins to figure out whether a wine is dry. How can something like the merlot not be sweet when they know, from tasting it, that it is sweet? How can an expert argue with their experience, from a reality that they know to be true? That this reality is a function of their brain rewiring their tastebuds never occurs to them. And, frankly, why should it? Most wine drinkers aren't neuro-scientists. Another way to look at this is to consider a glass of plain iced tea. That's dry, since it isn't sweet. Add lemon juice to the tea, and it becomes fruity, but still dry. Now add sugar to the iced tea, and it becomes fruity and sweet. The principle is the same with wine, and it really is that simple.

Wine's sweetness is measured by a concept called residual sugar, which means, literally, the sugar that is left over after fermentation. All wine, even the driest reds, has some residual sugar, since some sugars can't be converted to alcohol. Don't let the concept of fermentation intimidate you, either. It's very similar to bread baking. In bread, the yeast eats the sugar in the flour and the reaction produces carbon dioxide, which makes the loaf rise. It also produces tiny amounts of alcohol, which evaporate during baking. In wine, the yeast eats the sugar in the grape juice and converts it to alcohol; the carbon dioxide blows away.

The winemaker has two choices during fermentation: first, to let it go to the end, when the yeast eats all the sugar it can and then dies, or second, to stop fermentation early, before the yeast eats all the sugar. This leaves the wine a certain sweetness, depending how when the winemaker stops fermentation. Stopping it later means the wine won't be as sweet as stopping it earlier. Residual sugar is given as a percentage or as grams of sugar per liter; most wines with .8 percent residual sugar or less are dry (or 8 grams of sugar per liter for the technically-minded), and those with a higher number are sweet. Or, looking at it another way, wines with less alcohol (the cutoff is usually around 11 percent) are sweeter than higher alcohol wines.

This is not a difficult concept to understand, though it's one of those things that the wine business would prefer not to talk about, even for wines that are made to be sweet. Legally, wine must list its alcohol content, but trying to find the residual sugar level is much more difficult, even for professionals. It's rarely given on the label; when it is, it's either given as a percentage or as the afore-mentioned grams of sugar per liter, and how many consumers will know what that means? Some rieslings, in one of those developments that make me think there is hope for consumers, use a sweetness scale to describe how much sugar is in the wine, but that's an exception.

Producers are reluctant to let consumers know a wine's sweetness for three reasons. First, there is the idea, which the producers have promoted for much of the past 30 years, that sweet wine is somehow inferior, and that the less said about how sweet the wine is, the better. In the last couple of years, when the industry scored sales hits with sweet red wines like Apothic and Cupcake Red Velvet, they made sure to call them red blends for just that reason. Second, because sweetness levels vary so widely. A white zinfandel, the most common American sweet wine between the mid-1980s and the early 2000s, can have twice as much residual sugar as a dry wine or even one of the new sweet reds. And some of the new sweet wines, like red moscatos, are twice as sweet as white zinfandel. Who would knowingly buy a wine that said it had 14 percent residual sugar — more than 17 times the sweetness level of a dry red and three percentage points more than a 12-ounce serving of Coca-Cola?

The third reason? The trend in California to add sugar (in the form of grape juice concentrate) to dry wines after fermentation is complete. Winemakers do this because they want higher alcohol levels, which they see as a way to get better reviews from the Winestream Media. The problem is that high alcohol can be unpleasant in wine, producing the so-called hot sensation, an almost spirits-like feeling in the mouth more typically associated with scotch or bourbon. Adding grape juice can mitigate the hotness in the same way adding sugar makes a salad vinaigrette less vinegary. Mix the oil and vinegar and taste it, and then add a little sugar and taste it again. The sugar takes the edge off the vinegar and rounds out the flavors. The catch, of course, is that wineries that make wine this way and listed the residual sugar on the label would have 15 percent alcohol wines — a very high number — with as much residual sugar as some sweet reds. That would not be good for business. In fact, this is already happening with some sweet whites, which have 13 ½ or 14 percent alcohol and as much or more sweetness as a white zinfandel — which is only 11 percent or so alcohol. In this, they more resemble bottled cocktails than wine.

No doubt Rumpole would disapprove. Not because he would judge others by their wine, but because those wine drinkers weren't being treated fairly or honestly by the producers. Or, as he explained more than once when business was slow and he needed a client to defend: He needed more money to pay for the life-giving properties of Pommeroy's Very Ordinary Claret.

Chapter IV

How to buy cheap wine: The basics

There is no safe place to really learn about wine. There aren't any places where you can ask a stupid question. If you ask a question, it's as if the attitude is, 'Why don't you know this already?' instead of 'Why would you know this?' Because wine is so complicated, and there is so much to learn and who has the time to figure all this out?
— Allison Davis, TheHairpin blog

Allison Davis, a 20-something film and TV writer, didn't set out to be the voice of wine's lost generation. All she wanted to do, she said, was to air her frustration at wine's closed world, where the barriers include language, in which you have to know winespeak to make sense of what's going on, and class, because the impression is that only rich people can enjoy wine. Hence her post on TheHairpin, a blog aimed at Davis and people like her, and which gets more than 300,000 visitors a month. Which, ironically, are more people than all but a handful of Internet wine sites get, including WineSpectator.com.

"I got the feeling there was a sense of relief after I wrote the post," says Davis. "People were saying, 'I'm not the only one who feels this way.' You think everyone knows more about wine than you do when you're in your 20s. People don't trust themselves. They don't know what good wine is and what it's supposed to taste like."

Relief, indeed. The post was a huge sensation on TheHairpin, eliciting some 300 comments that asked almost every conceivable question about wine and that took the discussion into a variety of wine-related topics. To put that number in perspective: It's about as many as TheHairpin post about "accidental" bra touching got, and 10 times more than most posts on the most popular wine blogs get.

What does it say about wine that Davis' post on a blog aimed at young women without kids who have money — the kind of audience that makes advertisers drool — was so popular? It says that wine, at best, ignores its audience, and at worst takes it for granted. Or, as Davis wrote, she and her friends and millions of other wine drinkers, male and female, young and old, end up "smiling through a glass of something at a dinner party that [they] can't pronounce and aren't sure if [they're] supposed to enjoy, instead of actually enjoying the wine."

That's because the wine business doesn't care if its customers understand how to buy its product. Its success is not predicated on education, but on tradition and a 1950s way of doing things. Trust us, they say — believe what we've written on the back label no matter how silly it sounds, have faith that the name we've chosen and the cute puppy or kitty or whatever on the front label means quality, and don't worry about all that other stuff that we don't talk about, like the relationship between where the wine is from and how much it costs or that blended wine can be just as cheap and tasty as varietal wine. What you don't know makes it easier for us to make money.

Or, as one wine marketing consultant told me when we talked about this, "This is the only consumer goods product in the world that doesn't want to make things easier for its customers. If it did, every bottle of wine would have a screwcap. Can you imagine any other product making it harder for its customers to use it?"

Retailer as friend

Of course not. They make it easier, as beer and ketchup and laundry detergent and who knows what else have done — the screw-off beer top, the measuring cup as detergent cap. But what else to expect from an industry that, as Davis' lament about stupid questions demonstrates, makes it difficult to learn even the most basic concepts?

Fortunately, there is a solution, and it's as close as your local retailer. Perhaps the only good thing about three-tier and the 1950s-style wine sales model that still exists because of three-tier is that the system has protected the independent retailer. Local music and book stores may be gone, victims of retail consolidation and the Internet, but the laws that make it difficult to buy wine that you want when you want it have also kept small retailers in business. In some states, including New York, that's all there are — grocery stores that sell wine and chain liquor stores are illegal.

And that's usually where customer service still matters. Those retailers understand that customer service means answering stupid questions — it's their reason for being. This doesn't mean that all retailers are created equal, and that a local store is going to be more customer-friendly than a national chain, but given the way customer service works, it's more likely. Customer service is more important to retailers who can't compete on price, and most small retailers can't match what grocery stores, warehouse clubs, and the growing number of regional liquor chains charge for wine. The reason is economies of scale; bigger retailers, who order more, can get better pricing from distributors. It's not so much that national supermarket chains, the Cost Plus World Markets of the world, and warehouse stores like Costco don't care about customer service (that's a discussion that has been going on for decades), but that they understand that they'll sell wine even without it. They know that if their prices are lower, customers will trade service for saving money.

But saving money on some unknown wine doesn't help answer stupid questions, and Davis is far from the only person who has been overwhelmed by the great wall of bottles that make up a grocery store or warehouse store wine department. So consumers are forced to buy wine based on whether it has a cute label, how much it costs, and if the back label charms them into thinking the wine tastes like a cherry chocolate cupcake. None of these, obviously, are dependable indicators of quality.

Hence the need for a retailer who is dependable and who has the patience to help you find and understand quality. That's because the best retailers do more than sell wine. They help you find wine that you didn't know you would like. It's easy to sell someone something that they already know about. What's more difficult, and a mark of the best retailers, is to find something new that fits the parameters of wine they already like — a Spanish albarino or French picpoul for an Italian pinot grigio, for example, or a fruity rose for a white zinfandel.

How can you tell if you have a first-class retailer? Ask yourself these questions:

- Does the retailer ask questions about your preferences, helping you figure out what you want — red or white, sweet or dry? Or do they steer you to something they assume you'll like? This often happens with female customers; too many retailers assume they want something sweet and cute,

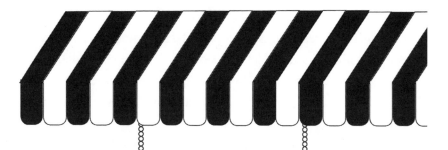

How to tell a good wine shop from bad

Does the retailer ask questions about your preferences, helping you figure out what you want – red or white, sweet or dry?

Does the retailer always seem to recommend wine that is on sale, is displayed at the end of an aisle, or highlighted in some other way – regardless of what you like?

Does the retailer let you ask questions? Do you feel comfortable asking those questions, and not as if you're being humored in the way adults humor small children?

Does the retailer answer your questions? Are the answers understandable or in winespeak?

and send them to that part of the store without a second thought. One woman, who helped me with a post for my blog about customer service, asked a salesman at a national chain about rose and left the store with white zinfandel.

- Does the retailer always seem to recommend wine that is on sale, is displayed at the end of an aisle, or highlighted in some other way — regardless of what you like? Many bigger retailers offer incentives to their employees if they meet sales goals or quotas on featured wines, and too often, that takes precedence over what the customer wants. One nationally known wine critic told me a San Francisco wine shop had very ordinary $45 pinot noir marked down to $36, and every time he tried to buy something else, the retailer steered him back to the pinot noir. The point being, of course, that this can happen to everyone, regardless of wine knowledge.

- Does the retailer let you ask questions? Do you feel comfortable asking those questions, and not as if you're being humored in the way adults humor small children?

- Does the retailer answer your questions? Are the answers understandable or in winespeak? And, when you say you don't understand what he or she means by leathery or oaky, do they smile and explain what they mean in English? Or do you get The Look that makes consumers like Davis crazy?

It's the real estate

Customer service, then, should be about education as much as where in the store something is located — what does the wine taste like, why is it different from another wine, and where is it from? In this, the idea of a wine's place is crucial in understanding how to buy the best cheap wines. At its most basic, it's about a wine term called appellation, which signifies where the grapes were grown that were used to make the wine — most broadly, in a country, and then more specifically, in a specific region within that country. That could mean France or California, or Bordeaux within France or Napa Valley within California. Appellation can get much more complicated, with sub-appellations within sub-appellations, so that a California wine from Napa Valley could then be from Howell Mountain and even from a vineyard with its own particular characteristics within Howell Mountain. Think of it as a pyramid — the country is at the base, and the various smaller classifications and sub-classifications sit on top of each other all the way to the top.

Each wine-producing region in the world uses some form of the appellation model, and most of them are based on the 150-year-old French system. Like the original French Bordeaux classification of 1855 and the later *appellation d'origine contrôlé*, or AOC, appellation is regulated by national governments, and there are strict standards about what qualifies as an appellation. The idea in defining appellation is typicity, where wines made from grapes in an appellation have certain things in common and a certain style.

In the U.S., the federal Treasury Department regulates appellation, called American Viticultural Areas, or AVAs. The U.S. has about 210 AVAs, almost half of them are not in California (and there are more than 3,200 appellations and regions worldwide). If a wine has a county, state, or country appellation, like Lake Country, California, or France, then at least 75 percent of the grapes used to make it must come from that county, state, or country. The standard is 85 percent for an appellation like Napa Valley or Bordeaux.

Appellation, as originally intended by the French, was a way to determine quality, and quality would then set price. Theoretically, quality is as simple as the quality of the grapes, and the more precise and prestigious the appellation (those regions nearest the top of the pyramid), the better the grapes. That meant the quality

How wine
appellations work

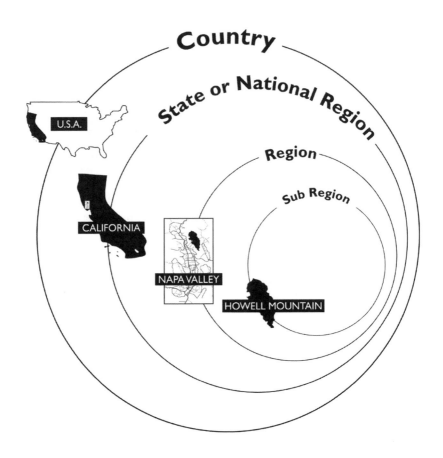

Country

State or National Region

Region

Sub Region

U.S.A.

CALIFORNIA

NAPA VALLEY

HOWELL MOUNTAIN

of the grapes usually determined the quality of the wine, and this was usually true from the early days of appellation in the 19th century well into the last quarter of the 20th century.

In other words, a wine with a California appellation doesn't come from a region as precise as a wine from Napa Valley, and that same Napa Valley wine doesn't come from a region as precise as Howell Mountain. The logic here is that the grapes in each smaller and better defined region are supposed to be of better quality and more representative of that region than the larger and less precise region underneath it in the pyramid. But, given the revolution in winemaking techniques and mindset over the past several decades, appellation is gradually becoming just another guideline in determining quality, save for the most prestigious regions. Improved technology, new growing techniques, better understanding of soil types, and experience over decades of harvests, as opposed to years, have improved the quality of the grapes in the appellations at the bottom of the pyramid. So a California wine is not necessarily going to be inferior to a wine from a more specific and precise appellation the way it would have been 10 or 20 years ago. For another, winemakers have become more skilled at mixing and matching grapes from higher and lower quality appellations to improve quality, another technique that was little used or understood before the end of the 20th century. Why would anyone want to use grapes from a more precise region in a wine with a California appellation? Because, as it turns out, using just a little of the former helps to make the latter a significantly better product, but doesn't much raise the price — yet another tool that could be used to boost the quality of cheap wine.

The other problem with appellation is that it was never intended to define value in the way value is defined today, where consumers want more quality than what they paid for. The cost of wine and its value were interchangeable, and this was one of the goals of the first appellation law in France. "Good" wine was expensive, "bad" wine was cheap, and there wasn't much room for discussion. Periodically, wine drinkers would return from Europe with near-mythical stories about the cheap table wine they bought at a corner grocer in Paris or drank at a trattoria outside of Rome and how wonderful it was. But these reports, like turning lead into gold, seemed too good to be true and served mainly as another example of just how much more fun wine was elsewhere than in the United States.

Also, this helps to explain why consumer-focused wine education has traditionally been so poor. No one thought there was a need for it, since it was obvious that "good" wine cost more money, and what else did the consumer need to know? The industry even prided itself on this. Unlike other consumer goods, you got what you paid for with wine. Thirty years ago, wine didn't have any foolishness like designer jeans, in which consumers paid more for a product that wasn't any better but was marketed more effectively to increase demand for the product.

But value has become part of the wine marketplace, much to the industry's chagrin and even disbelief. Consumers had been slowly moving toward value before the 2007-2010 recession, making best-sellers out of Big Wine products like Barefoot and Two-buck Chuck that were cheap and professionally made and that didn't exist before the revolution in technology that made them possible. The recession made value all powerful, breaking what was left of the connection between price and quality — or, as I wrote at the time, "$10 wine is the new $100 wine." The numbers were amazing — wine sales by bottles sold actually increased a little during the worst recession in 40 years, but sales measured in dollar terms declined by about the same amount. Consumers traded down and discovered value, along with something they did not expect, quality. This is borne out by a 2012 report from the

Wine Market Council, which studies consumer buying and consumption habits. More than 9 of 10 what the council calls core wine drinkers, those who buy most of the wine in the U.S., said it's possible to buy good wine without spending a lot of money. "The most desirable characteristics in a wine bought at retail are value, high quality, previous trial, and a high level of comfort when serving it to friends," said the report.

Defining value

What's even better, for people who care about value, is that the term is not difficult to define, despite its relatively short history as part of the wine lexicon. A wine provides value if it gives the drinker more — more quality, more fun, more pleasure, more wine-ness — than it costs. You can usually tell value on the first sip. If you swallow and smile, that's value. If you swallow and say to yourself, "What was I thinking when I bought this?" that's not value. And that's just as true for a cheap wine as an expensive one.

A French wine term called *terroir* goes a long way toward explaining why cheap wine is cheap, why some cheap wine doesn't taste cheap, and what determines value. *Terroir* is the thread that links winemaking around the world, whether a $5,000 bottle of Chateau Petrus from France or a $7 bottle of YellowTail merlot from Australia. The former tastes the way it does because the winemaker wants it to reflect its *terroir*, while the latter tastes the way it does because a decision has been made that *terroir* doesn't matter — or, more accurately, that *anti-terroir* is just as sound a way of making wine. And yes, it's not unlike matter and antimatter for anyone who understands particle physics or "Star Trek."

Terroir, at its most basic, doesn't have an exact English translation. It's usually literally and narrowly defined as something like "of the soil." The French understand *terroir* in this first and most limiting sense. For them, *terroir* is defined by where the grapes are grown, and that this difference in geography is basis for explaining what wine tastes like. In this, *terroir* is mostly about soil and everything that makes up the soil — different soil types, its composition, drainage, and the like. Call this the scientific approach to *terroir*, because the soil in Bordeaux is different from the soil in Burgundy. This means one region can have many *terroirs*, so that the Left Bank of Bordeaux can be different from the Right Bank, and parts of the Right Bank can be different from other parts of the Right Bank, and so on down to differences within the same vineyard. In this, the French use *terroir* as a noun: "The *terroir* of that vineyard is quite impressive."

The second definition of *terroir* is more encompassing, and is why the word is so difficult to translate; that is, that *terroir* includes not just a region's soil, but its weather, tradition, winemaking and vineyard management techniques, and history. In the French region of Alsace, for example, a winemaker can go to the University of Bordeaux or the University of California-Davis and learn every single modern winemaking technique, skill, and *raison d'etre* for using them. But in the end, he or she is an Alsatian winemaker, and every wine made will filter that new knowledge through their Alsatian background. It's hundreds of years of accumulated wisdom (and non-wisdom, as well), passed down from generation to generation — about making wine in a certain style, about how to work with the peculiarities of the soil, how to handle the unique weather and climate, how to deal with pests, and how to approach the grapes in the vineyard (cropping, canopy management, and a bunch of other very nerdy viticultural grape-growing stuff). Hence, an Alsatian who made chardonnay in California would make California chardonnay with an Alsatian twist — which would be especially interesting, since Alsace doesn't produce chardonnay.

British wine writer Jamie Goode calls this *terroir* as philosophy, and it does a better job of explaining why chardonnay from Burgundy tastes different from chardonnay from Australia, and why chardonnay from California tastes different again, than the first definition does. That's because there is more to winemaking than just the type of soil (though Goode, interestingly, believes in the first definition).

What's important here is not which definition is correct, but that if *terroir* exists, so does anti-*terroir* — the idea that wine doesn't have to take into account where it came from and that it should, as one of its most fervent proponents wrote in the Los Angeles Times newspaper several years ago, just taste good. All of the business about the soil is so much silliness, and wine doesn't necessarily have to be any different from ketchup in the way it's made. If the technology exists to make every bottle of wine taste exactly the same, and it does, then the best wine should be made that way. Why should the consumer suffer poorly-made wine to please a bunch of wine geeks? Oddly, even more traditional wine critics are being won over to the anti-*terroir* side (though they are usually more measured about it). Paul Lukacs, one of the most respected wine writers in the country and author of *Inventing Wine: A New History of one of the World's Most Ancient Pleasures,* argues that *terroir* originated as a marketing tool in the early 20th century, and there is as much myth as truth to it.

In many ways, anti-*terroir* — call it the international style of winemaking — explains why the quality of cheap wine is better than ever. The anti-*terroir* approach allows winemakers, and especially those who work for Big Wine, to use technology to smooth out the rough edges — too harsh tannins or too much acid (or not enough) or even a red wine that is too light in color — without worrying if they're making a wine from Argentina taste like a wine from the Paso Robles region of California. Which is a thought that makes *terroir* advocates flee in panic to the nearest basement to hide until the apocalypse is over.

Wine by formula

Anti-*terroir* does two other things, which is one reason why it's so popular with Big Wine. First, it enables wine to be made to a formula so that it tastes the same every time, regardless of vintage or weather or soil. The wine industry has always been able to enhance what the harvest has given it, going back hundreds of years. That most people don't know about this isn't surprising; it's another of those things that the wine business doesn't like to talk about. The German, French, and even the Italians have long practiced chaptalization, in which some kind of sugar is added during the winemaking process to enrich the wine, making it taste fruitier and boosting the alcohol content. This was sometimes necessary in cooler climates, when the grapes didn't ripen enough. Without chaptalization, which helped power fermentation, the wine would be thin and bitter.

The difference between then and now is that chaptalization is child's play. Wine not dark enough in color because the grapes didn't ripen correctly? Then add Mega Purple, a grape juice concentrate made from a couple of little known wine grapes and that is completely natural (since it's grape juice) to boost the color, a practice not uncommon in grocery store pinot noir. Want to keep the added fruit flavors of higher alcohol wines, but don't want the higher alcohol, like in some grocery store zinfandels? Then spin the wine, a distilling process that separates some of the volatile compounds and some of the alcohol from the grape juice, and allows the winemaker to add the volatile compounds back to the juice without the alcohol. Hence, high alcohol flavor without the high alcohol. Wine not tannic enough naturally? Then add liquid tannins, which come in assorted flavors, like toasted oak.

And then there is the technology to replace oak aging, which has been a hallmark of the best and most expensive red and white wines for centuries. Oak aging takes place after fermentation is complete, when the wine is transferred to oak barrels about the size of a couple of home office filing cabinets. Oak aging, through a series of chemical reactions, softens the wine's tannins and makes it richer and more complex, adding flavors and aromas (vanilla, for example, and the infamous toasty and oaky). The catch is that oak aging is expensive, not only from the cost of the barrels, but from the time it takes to age the wine properly, which can be as long as two years. Because, if the wine is aging in a barrel, it's not on a store shelf bringing cash to the winery.

So what do winemakers do who want oak's advantages without the added cost and time? Add wood chips or dominoes to the wine after it has fermented, or age the wine in a steel tank or old barrel with oak staves attached the inside of the tank. These substitutes have been around for decades, and were often illegal to use. But as the laws changed, the chip technology improved. Plus, they can cost a tenth as much as a barrel and come in a variety of flavors and styles. Want to add a cinnamon note to your wine? There's a chip for that. Want the equivalent of an oak barrel with heavy toast, which means the inside is charred by hand with a torch and is usually only possible with a barrel that can cost thousands of dollars? There's a chip for that.

Second, this technology allows Big Wine (and a lot of so-called boutique and artisan wineries, if the truth be known) to make wine based on consumer taste profiles or high score criteria, something that has never really been possible in wine's 1,500-year history. There's even a California company, Enologix, that has analyzed high-scoring wines for tannin content, ripeness, and even more technical qualities, and can recommend how a winery can manipulate its grapes to to make a wine that will get similar high scores.

Before this advanced technology, wine drinkers drank what the grapes and climate gave them, and if the wine was too tannic or too sweet or not acidic enough, then it was called a bad vintage and everyone waited for next year. Typically, the most common sweet table wines were rieslings, almost all red wine was dry, white wine had less alcohol than red and most table wine didn't have a lot of alcohol, and there wasn't much anyone could do about it. There's no need for that anymore; just hold a focus group and find out what consumers want. They don't like tannins? Then make the tannins less noticeable, using a technique called micro-oxygenation. They want a sweet wine, but one that still has some of the attributes of a dry wine? Then make a dry wine, but add grape juice concentrate to the almost finished product, and the wine will be slightly sweet but with a dry red's alcohol content and mouth feel — or, as consumers say, smooth and fruity.

Another irony in the *terroir* debate is that wine geeks have rarely included cheap wine in their discussions. Anti-*terroir* might be the spawn of the devil, but only for wines that matter — not the junk that the rest of us drink. In this, *terroir* was widely accepted until the 1990s, when wine critic Robert Parker started giving some of his best scores to wines — no matter where they came from — that were richer and more concentrated and as high in alcohol as possible. Parker almost certainly didn't set out to discover anti-*terroir*; all he did was score wines highly that he thought were well made, and he happened to like a certain style that didn't depend on the traditional definition of *terroir*. Plus, his palate and its influence coincided with the revolution in wine technology that made it possible to make wine that didn't depend on *terroir*. The rest is history, and so much so that French wine consultant and anti-*terroir* guru Michel Rolland never met a wine he couldn't make rich, concentrated, and over-ripe, no matter where it was from and no matter the *terroir* (in either definition), and his disciples are widely spread across the wine industry. Rolland, for example, makes a $20 Argentine wine called Clos de los Siete that is technically brilliant. How else to describe a wine from Argentina that tastes like it came from Paso Robles, thousands of miles away and just as different in *terroir*? But, as the *terroirists* howl (and with some justification), wine is not ketchup and should not be made that way. Technically brilliant is sometimes not enough.

Does *terroir* matter for cheap wine? The answer is no — except when it does. Is it possible to make perfectly acceptable cheap wine that uses the latest technology to turn ordinary grapes into something that may be more than ordinary and a value to boot? Of course. Because, as has been noted on these pages countless times, that has been Big Wine's greatest contribution, and consumers don't have to suffer poorly-made cheap wine any more. If you have $10, or even $8 or $6, then there is a wine you can drink that won't disappoint you, and it doesn't matter if its appellation isn's prestigious or if it doesn't have a vintage. You don't need to know about *terroir* or care about it or even believe in it to drink cheap wine, because Big Wine has eliminated the worry.

Location, location, location

But there is more to cheap wine than something that is merely professional or sound, and its goal should be more than not disappointing — just like expensive wine is supposed to be. Cheap wine can reflect *terroir*, and most of the wines in the $10 Hall of Fame, which appears every January on the Wine Curmudgeon blog, are *terroir*-driven. They are made by winemakers and producers who respect that sense of place and who don't see a wine's price as limiting the role *terroir* plays. Those are the best cheap wines, whether they come from places where *terroir* is almost taken for granted, like California and France, or regions that once were limited by their *terroir* and have since learned how to use it to their advantage, like Sicily and parts of Spain.

Which brings the discussion back to appellation. No matter what else you hear and no matter what the Winestream Media preaches, the most important factor in determining a wine's price is where its grapes were grown. Again, this rarely has anything to do with value or quality. Appellation, which in its original 19th century French incarnation equated cost with quality and value, has morphed into a way to define price, where the cost of the land determines the price of the wine — the less expensive the land, the less expensive the wine. Yes, there are exceptions to this, and the wine industry will howl and insist it's not true, but that's why a wine with a California appellation is less expensive than a wine with a more precise sub-appellation, like Napa, and why that wine is usually less expensive again than a wine with an even more precise sub-appellation, like Howell Mountain. This principle holds true for every wine-producing region in the world.

This can't be repeated often enough. The most expensive land does not necessarily produce grapes that make the "best" wine, just as the least expensive land does not produce grapes that make the "worst" wine. Buying vineyard land, like buying a house, does not adhere to a rational, sensible, Economics 101 pattern. Why would anyone want to pay $2,000 a month to rent a 900-square foot apartment in Manhattan when they can buy a house that is twice as big, with a yard, for the same monthly payment in Dallas? But they do, because they see a reason for it, be it culture or vibe or whatever, and the cost of vineyard land in the 21st century often follows the same logic.

First is supply and demand. Vineyard land in Napa Valley can cost as much as $300,000 an acre, but not necessarily because it's some of the best vineyard land in the world. Demand for Napa land drives the cost up, because so many people want to own a winery there and there isn't a lot of it — in other words, just like the Manhattan real estate market. The best Napa land is twice as expensive as in next-door Sonoma, but are Napa wines always twice as good? Of course not. Second is the on-going cost of the land. Some European vineyard land has been in the same family for generations (if not longer), and the land itself doesn't cost anything any more in terms of production. It was paid for long ago. This is one reason why some Alsatian and Burgundian wines from France, though expensive, are much better values than comparable wines from Napa, despite currency fluctuations and the cost of transporting them across the Atlantic Ocean. Every month, a Napa winery pays a lender principle and interest to cover land costs that these European producers don't have to pay.

How screwy is all this cost business? Consider that if production costs account for one-fifth of the price of bottle of a wine (from the chart in Chapter I), and using some very rough math that takes into account the production techniques used at a high-end Napa winery and allowing for other production costs, the cost of Napa land, translated into the cost of the grapes that go into the wine, can add as much as $50 to $100 to the price of a bottle of wine. Whether it does or not is one of those hard business decisions that a winery owner has to make, even if he or she may not have known that when they thought buying a winery would be fun.

This does not mean that Napa wine with a $100 a bottle land cost isn't a great wine and unworthy of rhapsodic prose. It means that it may not necessarily be a value, and that's the point of this discussion. It's not difficult to make great wine when price is no object; what's more difficult is to make great wine within the constraints of a budget and limited resources. And, since land cost is the most important constraint, the best values usually come from regions where land is less expensive, whether there is less demand for the land or because there are fewer on-going costs.

Value and price

The one place where there is almost never any value, unless you're buying the most expensive bottle, is on a restaurant wine list. This doesn't matter if you're at a national chain, where a $7 bottle of white zinfandel can cost as much as $25, or at a high-end local restaurant, where $100 might buy a very ordinary bottle of Champagne. Most restaurants don't understand what do with wine; they see it as inventory that needs to be expensed instead of an asset that needs to be sold. In one respect, this is understandable — people go into the restaurant business to sell food and not wine, and the overwhelming majority of a chef's training is in food and not wine. The difficulty, though, is that the restaurant business wants us to believe they're serious when they're just paying lip service to the idea of wine and as part of eating at a restaurant.

Hence the notorious three-to-one markup, where almost every bottle that comes in is sold for three times what it costs, the exception being the most expensive bottles, which are sometimes marked up only two to one. Or the poor level of employee wine training, where the staff often seems to know as little about what's on the wine list as the customer does, and are too often snotty about what they do know. Or the flawed and oxidized wine that is sold every day because no one knows it has gone bad and should be thrown out. Or out-of-date wine lists, where the restaurant never seems to have anything other than the most popular wines in stock. Or crappy wine lists, where the wines were chosen by the distributor as part of a promotion to place the company's wines in the restaurant.

This does not mean that there aren't exceptions. More chains, including places like Olive Garden, see wine as a way to make a $10 spaghetti dinner into something more, and have increased the quality of the wine they sell and improved employee training. Half-price wine promotions are more common than ever. Younger and more progressive sommeliers who have been trained in wine and the needs of restaurants have more influence at increasing numbers of high-end operations. But the majority, unfortunately, haven't changed.

The value/price tradeoff

$12 or less

$12 to $18

$18 to $30

Really Expensive

More value than any other price category

Less value than the first group and not much overall – the province of Big Wine marketing

More value than you'd expect, especially from the Old World

Really expensive: Hardly any value at all; these are wines you drink for no other reason than they're terrific.

PRICE VS QUALITY

Restaurant bosses would never treat a chicken breast the way they treat a bottle of wine, because they know no one would eat an overpriced piece of poor quality chicken that has gone off. But they think nothing of doing this with wine. I've watched a waitress try to open a bottle of wine by putting it between her legs to pull the cork out. I've had a waiter (more than one, actually) argue with me about whether a wine was oxidized, insisting that it was perfectly fine and I should shut up and drink it. Or, even worse, look at me quizzically because they didn't know what oxidized meant. I've had any number of bartenders tell me that the wine I was drinking was the correct temperature, even though it was red and chilled or white and warm or vice versa.

And nothing seems to change this. Television exposes haven't helped, like the CNN survey a couple of years ago that claimed markups of as much as 500 percent wasn't unusual. Academic studies haven't helped, like the Cornell University report several years ago that said wine prices were too high and hurt sales. Restaurants just aren't interested in doing things differently, and there are few ways around high restaurant wine prices.

Fortunately, the situation is different at retail. The wine on store shelves fits into four broad price categories — $12 or less, $12 to $18, $18 to $30, and really expensive. There are wonderful wines in the first group and most of the value; much less value in the second group, probably because producers don't improve the quality of the wine as much as they increase the price and gussy up the label; a lot of terrific wines in the third group and even some value; and not enough wine in the fourth group that most of us would drink if we had to pay for it. Besides, value in a $100 wine is a metaphysical question that, like Camus' Sisyphus and the boulder he must always roll up the hill, has no answer.

Since value depends on quality, determining which regions provide the best combination of price and value is subject to constant change. Two decades ago, Beaujolais in France offered unsurpassed value; today, the wines are too often tired and worn out, and aren't much of a value even when they're cheap. A decade ago, Chile was the world's unsurpassed value leader, and many of its sauvignon blancs were stunning $10 wines. But quality suffered as the country's producers boosted production to meet increased demand — a sad and familiar refrain in cheap wine.

It's also worth noting that popularity doesn't translate to value, and this is more than being a snob. Millions of cases of cheap Italian pinot grigio and Argentine malbec are imported into the U.S. every year, and consumers usually get their money's worth. But that's not the same as getting value — or, as the wine industry calls it, making wines that under-promise and over-deliver. In addition, it's possible to find cheap wines with value in regions that are dominated by more expensive wines, like the Rhone and Bordeaux in France. But it's more difficult than looking at a list to find these wines, and requires a fair amount of trial and error, also known as buying and drinking.

California, not surprisingly, is a special case for a couple of reasons. First, less popular regions with cheaper land, like Lodi, produce some amazingly over-priced wines where value was never intended to be part of the product. Second, most California appellation grocery store wines are nothing more than drinkable and consumer-friendly, despite the efforts of top-flight value producers like McManis and Bogle. Here, more ironies abound. Pine Ridge in Napa Valley makes a fabulous $10 white wine blend, which seems odd given that its reason for being is a $150 cabernet sauvignon. And Pine Ridge is far from an exception — see Wente, Dry Creek, and Robert Hall, among others. The rule then, for California? It's more about producer than appellation; if a producer does expensive wine, then their cheap wines usually offer plenty of value. Keep that in mind when you find a trusted retailer. It should be one of the first questions to ask.

Regions that offer the most value in $10 wine

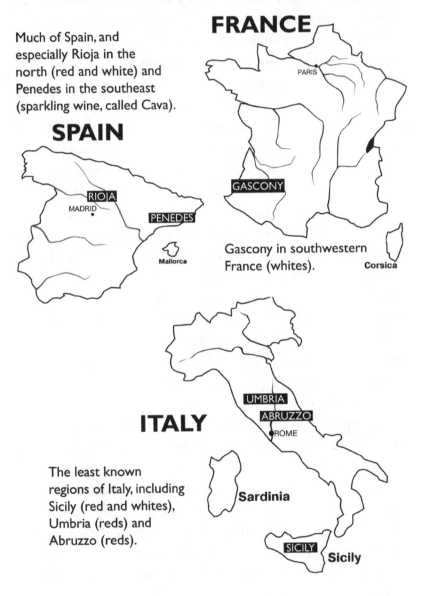

Much of Spain, and especially Rioja in the north (red and white) and Penedes in the southeast (sparkling wine, called Cava).

SPAIN

RIOJA
MADRID
PENEDES
Mallorca

FRANCE

PARIS

GASCONY

Gascony in southwestern France (whites).

Corsica

ITALY

UMBRIA
ABRUZZO
ROME

Sardinia

The least known regions of Italy, including Sicily (red and whites), Umbria (reds) and Abruzzo (reds).

SICILY
Sicily

So, allowing for these exceptions, these wine regions offer the best value, and especially in the $10 price range:

- Much of Spain, and especially Rioja in the north and Penedes in the northeast near Barcelona, for sparkling wine, called cava.
- Sicily in Italy, which has undergone perhaps the most impressive improvement in wine quality in the world. Just 20 years ago, the wines were old-fashioned and flawed; today, red and whites are distinctive, well-made, and tasty.
- Also in Italy — Umbria and Abruzzo, near Rome and among the country's least critically heralded regions. But the wines, mostly reds, are interesting and worth drinking.
- Gascony in southwestern France. Long known for cognac, a number of progressive Gascon winemakers have taken the grapes used for cognac to make cheap, delicious, white wines.

All of which means that Allison Davis has answers to her questions. Now it's time to start using the answers to find wines that she and the millions like her will like — without anyone making trouble for wine's lost generation.

Chapter V

How to buy cheap wine: Advanced course

> You've seen it—the way people in restaurants nervously pass round a wine list. It's fear. You as an industry have encouraged that fear. The wine industry is the most fragmented market I've seen. Fragmented, confusing, impenetrable.
>
> —Sir John Hegarty, British ad executive

A pparently, Sir John has tried to buy a bottle of wine at a U.S. retailer, and been overwhelmed by the number of bottles available. Or tried to decipher a back label, what with its buzzwords, hyperbole, and winespeak. Or tried to figure out the difference between a wine from Chile vs. a wine from Argentina vs. a wine from California without much help from the people who made them. Or tried to appreciate the difference between cabernet sauvignon and merlot, when both may be described by the same terms even though they're quite different wines. Or tried to have someone explain the difference between a varietal like cabernet and a blend in simple English. Or tried to reason why some foods go with some wines and some don't. Or, perhaps most frustratingly, tried to understand why a $25 wine is $25 and a $10 wine is $10 — without anything more to go on than descriptors that allude to poetry and romance instead of economic sense.

In which case, he's no different than the rest of us.

That's the irony. Hegarty is an insider who loves wine and owns a vineyard in the south of France, but also has a perspective that so many in the wine business lack. His 2010 speech to a group of British wine experts, for all practical purposes, ticked off each item that frustrates wine drinkers, both experienced and novice. "The [wine] industry fails hopelessly on accessibility," he told them. "This is a market that goes out of its way to confuse the consumer."

Hegarty was particularly vehement in his criticism of the wine business' insistence on pairing food and wine, which he argued is irrelevant in the 21st century and one of the reasons why so many wine drinkers are so intimidated. Want to make things easier? Then, he said, stop telling wine drinkers — no, ordering wine drinkers — what to pair with their dinner. Let them drink whatever they want.

Do they matter?

This is a revolutionary approach. Pairings have been an integral part of the wine business since at least the first part of the 20th century, and one can argue that the wine business that came of age in the U.S. in the 1980s did so around the idea of pairings. It offered structure and rules to guide consumers who wanted to try wine but had no idea what wine was, let alone what to buy. It's no coincidence that Blue Nun, a sweetish German riesling that was one of the most popular wines in the U.S. 40 years ago, made its mark with the slogan, "The white wine that's correct with any dish."

The wine pairing debate

No, because everyone experiences tastes differently, and what fits one person may not fit another

Yes, food and wine pairings matter because scientific studies have shown some food tastes better with some wine.

Only you can figure out if wine and food pairings make a difference

Pairings remain powerful. Amazon lists more than 1,300 books that deal with pairings, including titles from the popular "Dummies" and "Complete Idiots" series. By comparison, the online retailer lists fewer than 500 books about cheap wine. There are wine and food pairing websites (foodandwinepairing.org, matchingfoodandwine.com, wine-food-matcher.com); charts and graphics galore, including various versions of the legendary food pairing wheel, which is supposed to let you dial up a wine for any dish; and story after story in the Winestream Media delineating the rules for food and wine pairings, whether it's the Wine Spectator's six simple tips, Food and Wine's 15 rules, or recipes that best pair food and wine from the Wine Enthusiast. The accredited sommeliers who guard high-end restaurant wine lists must pass pairings tests to earn certification as either a master of wine or master sommelier.

Pairings can get even geekier, too, with chefs and sommeliers trying to outdo each other to match obscure wines with bizarre dishes, and then charging patrons hundreds of dollars a person to taste a natural wine paired with avocado and pancetta foam. Even those of us who know better have been sucked in. The final exam that I gave at the Dallas Le Cordon Bleu (I taught the wine class several years ago) asked the students to match food with wine. Most Americans, even if they know nothing else about wine, know two things: Drink red wine with meat and white wine with fish, and older wine is better than younger. That both aren't true is yet another example of the sorry state of wine education.

Yet no less than Auguste Escoffier, the patron saint of French cuisine, insisted on food and wine pairings in his classic *Le Guide Culinaire*, the cookbook that has been called the base that modern cuisine is built on. Escoffier's contention was that food tasted better with wines that complemented it, and he drew on his vast experience in late 19th and early 20th century kitchens to make his point. The man who invented the peach Melba dessert, a staple of 1950s home cookery that has long been out of favor, wasn't afraid to pair Champagne with an Asian-style salad made with pineapples, oranges, tomatoes, lettuce hearts, and fresh cream 100 years before anyone else thought of it. That's practically wine and foam territory.

This is something that the European wine business never doubted. There's a wine term, food wine, which is used to describe a wine that goes particularly well with food. These kinds of wines are made in such a way so they taste better with food than they do when you drink them by themselves. This approach, even without any real scientific proof, has been a staple of European winemaking for decades. Traditional Italian wine, with its high acid, is the best example. It tastes markedly different on its own than it does when paired with fatty foods like pork and cheese that are integral parts of the traditional Italian diet.

Research over the past century, including work done at the University of California-Davis, has tended to support these theories. Recently, a 2012 paper in the scientific journal Current Biology found that the way food feels in the mouth may make the biggest contribution to the phenomenon. The study found that wine, which is astringent, and meat, which is fatty, balance each other out. In the balance, the meat has a better mouthfeel and "tastes" better. Or, as the report concluded: "Repeatedly alternating samples of astringent beverages with fatty foods yielded ratings of fattiness and astringency that were lower than if rinsing with water or if presented alone without alternation."

Don't be intimidated by the jargon, for this is easy enough to test at home. Pick a dish, even something as simple as a hamburger or chicken salad. Taste the food with a sip of wine, a sip of sweet iced tea, a sip of soft drink, and a sip of water. See if there is a difference. Something about the wine meshes with the food, and the wine brings out flavors that don't seem to be there when you eat the food with the other liquids. One of the best examples is red wine with spaghetti and tomato sauce. The sugar in the tea and the soft drink overpower the tomato sauce, while the water doesn't do much of anything. The wine, though, somehow, makes the dish more complete.

Given all of this, why Hegarty's rant and the reaction against wine and food pairings? Because, like so many other things in wine (including scores), pairings assume everyone's tasting mechanism works the same way, and that what one person likes and dislikes holds true for everyone else. Which, despite the evidence that some sort of pairing relationship exists, is certainly not the case. There are too many variables involved, as noted in Chapter III. You like caviar, but I think it tastes like moldy fungus. I like baked beans with bacon, but you think it's too sweet and too greasy. So how can a one-size-fits-all explanation work for pairings?

That's the conclusion of Tim Hanni, a master of wine who has done extensive research in the field. His mantra: "Wine and food pairing is a fraud foisted on the unknowing. You want to pair wine with the diner, not the dinner." Hanni, over three decades of work with Cornell physician Virginia Utermolen, decided that people could be divided into four tasting groups, based on biology and behavior. It's not enough to understand how we taste physiologically, he said. We also need to understand how our experience tasting food affects what we like. This could explain, at its most basic, why people from cultures with spicy food tend to like spicy food more than people from cultures where spicy food isn't common. Or why some of us think raw fish tastes as good as anything we can eat and some of us think it tastes like raw fish. Or, given that Americans grew up drinking sweet tea and soft drinks, it's not surprising that many of them prefer sweet wine paired with food that is not classically paired with sweet wine.

retailer named Josh Wesson more than 20 years ago: "Would you eat vanilla ice cream, even if you didn't like it, because I told you to eat vanilla ice cream? Of course, not. You'd eat chocolate. Why should wine be any different?" The only thing that's required to take advantage of this flexibility is to realize there's a reason other people pair wine more traditionally. Make an effort to understand why someone else may find that the sweetness of the white zinfandel sours the flavors of the beef or that the powerful qualities in the red may overwhelm the delicacy of the fish.

At least wine drinkers have some sort of understanding of food and wine pairings, as complicated and convoluted as they may be. Too often, they have even less knowledge about the differences between varietal wines — wines made with one kind of grape, like cabernet sauvignon and chardonnay — and those made with combinations of grapes, like cabernet and merlot, called blends. This confusion is so widespread that some wine drinkers, raised on varietals, assume that blends are inherently inferior. John Bratcher, who has seen the American wine world evolve since the 1970s as retailer, winery executive, and wine broker, says it's not unusual to find wine drinkers who speak of blends with distaste, claiming that they are not only worse than varietals, but cheaper in the worst sense of the word. One man at a tasting, says Bratcher, told him in no uncertain terms that wineries used blends to dispose of their worst grapes. Bratcher asked him how he knew this, and the man said it was obvious, confirming the first rule of the wine snob: "I know something to be true without actually having to know anything about it."

So let's clear this up immediately: Blends produce some of the great wines of the world, and blends have been producing great wines for centuries. The most prestigious red wines of Bordeaux and the Rhone in France are blends, mostly cabernet and merlot in Bordeaux and syrah and a variety of less well-known grapes

Blended wine styles

Red Bordeaux: Cheap quality wines are hard to find; made primarily with cabernet sauvignon and merlot

White Bordeaux: More rare than red Bordeaux and still mostly made in Bordeaux, but produces excellent cheap wines made with sauvignon blanc and semillon

Red Rhone: Complicated combinations of of as many as 22 grapes (mostly syrah and grenache) that offer value and quality at the $10 level. Found worldwide.

White Rhone: Less common than red Rhone, but opportunity for $10 value and quality. Made worldwide, and mostly with viognier and combinations of lesser known grapes.

Super Tuscan: Red blend (sangiovese, cabernet, and merlot) that started in Italy and is sometimes made elsewhere. Usually expensive, but can provide excellent value at $10 or $12 regions other than Tuscany.

in the Rhone. Bends have also been important in the history of Spanish and Italian red wines, and it's almost impossible to make Champagne and other sparkling wines without blending grapes. Even the New World, from Australia to California, has embraced blends. And blends, frankly, can produce terrific cheap wine, since the process allows the winemaker to pick the best grapes for the money that he or she can find, regardless of varietal, and mix and match in the process until they find the optimum blend.

So, why the confusion? Two reasons: First, that Americans were taught to drink varietal wines in the 1980s, part of the fighting varietal movement (Chapter II) pioneered by a handful of California wineries. The industry spent a lot of time and money 30 years ago to convince wine drinkers that cabernet, chardonnay, and merlot were the best wines, and not the older blends that were made with grapes that no one had ever heard of. The irony was that the fighting varietals weren't necessarily better wines because they were varietals, but because the wineries had learned how to make better wine, regardless of the grapes being used. The second reason: That Americans didn't necessarily know they were drinking blends before the fighting varietals arrived. U.S. wines had names like chablis and hearty burgundy, both of which were blends and neither of which were made with grapes called chablis or burgundy.

That's because California mimicked the European practice of naming wines after the region where they came from, if not following it exactly. Producers figured that if they used European names for their wine, some of that cachet would rub off on a very uneducated wine drinking public. In retrospect, all it did was confuse wine drinkers then and now. For example, the French region of Burgundy produces chardonnay and pinot noir, but the wines are called white Burgundy and red Burgundy. And an Italian Chianti isn't made with the chianti grape, but comes from the Chianti region in Tuscany in northern Italy and made primarily with the sangiovese grape. This very brief explanation should go a long way towards explaining why European wine does such a good job of baffling beginning wine drinkers who have been brought up on varietals, and also why European producers have started in the last several years to put the name of the grape on their wine labels. The Europeans have acknowledged that it's easier to change a system that is hundreds of years old than to change the way American consumers identify wine.

Even more confusion

The final confusing note about blends: A varietal wine can be made with more than one grape, but still be called by its varietal name. That's because federal law, which even applies to imported wine, allows winemakers to add up to 25 percent of something else without calling it a blend, and most wine producing countries have similar laws. This means the cabernet sauvignon on the local store shelf could be made with one-quarter merlot or syrah, but the law doesn't require anyone to tell the consumer. For the most part, this isn't a problem, and producers even take a perverse pride in listing every grape that's part of the other 25 percent. This type of blending is usually done to improve the quality of the wine, in that adding merlot to cabernet will round out the rough edges and adding viogner to chardonnay will make the flavors brighter.

Blends are made everywhere in the world where wine is made, and winemakers pretty much blend anything with anything else these days. But there are several distinct styles, usually classified by the region in which they originated:

- Bordeaux: Red and white blends. The reds are mostly cabernet and merlot, though legally (yes, there are French laws limiting what grapes can be grown in which regions) three other red grapes can be used — malbec, petit verdot, and cabernet franc. Red Bordeaux blends are made worldwide, and price remains a guide to quality, with cheap quality wines difficult to find. The white blend (sauvignon blanc and semillon) is much more rare and still mostly comes from Bordeaux, but it's not hard to find, and produces excellent cheap wines that have citrus fruit and even minerality.

- Rhone: Red and white blends of combinations that can involves as many was 22 grapes and that almost require their own chapter. For one thing, white grapes are often used in red blends; for another, the laws in France (where the northern Rhone uses different grape combinations than the southern Rhone) don't apply elsewhere. The most common red grapes used for in these blends are syrah, grenache, and mourvedre, while the most common whites are viognier and roussanne. Rhone blends can offer value and quality, even at the $10 level, and are some of my favorites. French red Rhone blends are dark and earthy, while those made elsewhere (California and Australia, for example) are much fruitier. White Rhone blends from France can be almost oily, while those from Australia, California, and even South Africa are fresh and lively.

- Super Tuscan: This red blend of sangiovese, cabernet, and merlot is relatively new, created by producers in the Tuscany region who wanted to use grapes that weren't allowed under local appellation regulations. So they labeled it with the table wine appellation, and the blends have become popular in several other parts of Italy. The wines are usually expensive, but can provide excellent value at $10 or $12 from producers like Vitiano.

Two other kinds of wine that aren't thought of as blends, but often are, show how important blending is to the wine business. Champagne and sparkling wine are almost always made with more than one grape, and blending gives them their unique flavor (the bubbles come from another part of the winemaking process). The grapes used in the blend depend on which country the sparkling wine comes from, but that almost everyone blends champagne-style wines speaks to the key role blending plays. (Wine geek note: Only sparkling wine made in the Champagne region of France can be called Champagne, thanks to a series of trade agreements other wine countries have signed with the European Union. Even wine made in other regions of France can't be called Champagne.) The other blend often overlooked is rose, the pink wine that isn't sweet. Many roses are made from one grape, but many are made from more than one, especially in some of the best rose producing parts of the world like southern France and California.

Once a day

Which makes this the place to note that sparkling wine that isn't Champagne and rose offer some of the best cheap wine values in the world. Most wine drinkers, even experienced ones, don't think of the two as something to drink every day. The former, thanks to tradition and old-fashioned marketing designed to sell over-priced Champagne, is supposed to be saved for special occasions, while the latter is to be avoided because it resembles sweet wine like white zinfandel and its knockoffs. Real men don't drink pink, do they?

This is just more foolishness. Anyone who doesn't drink either kind of wine regularly (assuming they like it, of course) is missing out on some of the best cheap wine in the history of wine. The revolution in wine discussed in Chapter II has had tremendous impact on both kinds of wine, and especially on sparkling wine. It's cheaper, for one thing, so that $10 — or even less — buys a bottle that would have cost twice as much 20 years ago. And the quality is indescribably better. The bubbly stuff that tasted like 7-Up that people of a certain age will remember from weddings and anniversaries has been replaced by sparkling wines that are dry, crisp, and fruity, without any nasty sweetness. The Spanish led this turnaround with Cava, their version of sparkling wine, and the Italians have followed in the last decade with vastly improved Prosecco. Sparkling wine's other great attribute is that it's fun to drink, especially on a Tuesday night when you've had a long day and feel tired and cranky and the Chinese takeout you brought home is cold and gloppy. And, for those who wonder, it pairs with almost anything.

Rose is even more overlooked, though this is changing as younger wine drinkers enter the market. Older drinkers, who were brought up to dislike white zinfandel and have less than fond memories of sweet pink wines like Lancer's and Mateus, figure that because rose is pink, it must be the same thing. And it's not. Roses are usually made with red grapes (as discussed in Chapter II) that have qualities of both red and white wines — the color and fruit flavors of the former but without the tannins, and the acid and freshness of the later. Rose's fruit flavors are mostly red berries (think strawberry or cranberry) or watermelon. Styles vary by country, though these are becoming less noticeable as Big Wine's fruity style gains more influence. Traditionally, Spanish rose is bone dry with the least fruit flavor. French roses are not quite as dry as Spanish, but they usually don't have a lot of fruit flavor and often have minerality. Some U.S. roses are so full of strawberry flavor that they seem sweet, as was discussed in Chapter III. One caveat: Don't buy old rose. Look for vintages that are a year old, and at most two. Roses are not made to age, and should be fresh and flavorful. The color in older vintages starts to fade, like paper that yellows, and the taste does the same thing before eventually oxidizing (which means it picks up a brandy-like flavor).

The best thing about rose is the price. Very few cost more than $10 or $12, and even very ordinary cheap rose that has been dumbed down to the most basic Big Wine fruit-forward style isn't unpleasant, in the way that some cheap pinot grigio has an almost turpentine taste or some cheap malbec tastes like grape juice mixed with a little grain alcohol. At the worst, they're just not as enjoyable as more traditional roses. Chill them, even with an ice cube or two, and you have wine that is adequate for almost any occasion.

An ice cube? He's kidding, right? Not at all. This is exactly the point that Hegarty makes about wine's rules and regulations stifling wine drinking. That I can make a joke about ice cubes points to the seriousness with which the wine community takes its rules. One puts ice cubes in soft drinks, not wine, and this is usually said while giving the offender a penetrating glare. But why not ice cubes? Why not white zinfandel with prime rib? Why not whatever you want?

This is the question that the wine business has never answered, and the question that those of us who are passionate about wine and who want to share our passion want it to answer. And quickly. Because, until the question is answered, the wine business will never find its Holy Grail — the legendary and elusive gateway wine, the one that gets people interested in wine and that they use as a springboard to the rest of the wine world. What's the wine that will convince people who prefer beer or soft drinks that wine has something to offer them? This is not uncommon in many other consumer goods — teenagers starting out with a cheap used car who eventually drive something very sporty and photo enthusiasts who move from using their cell phones for taking pictures of themselves in the bathroom mirror to shooting with the snazziest rig they can afford.

But not wine. This doesn't happen in wine, and probably hasn't happened since the fighting varietal days of the 1980s — if it happened then. The statistics make this very clear. Per capita wine consumption in the U.S. more than doubled between 1966 and 1986, which marked the beginning of the revolution in wine quality. Since then, per capita wine consumption has remained relatively unchanged. There's no evidence that more Americans are drinking wine, and what evidence there is suggests that the growth in total consumption since 1986, about 45 percent, has come from people who were already drinking wine, the Wine Market Council's so-called core group.

How this has happened, despite what seems to be wine's increasing popularity, is one of the great empty spaces in the study of wine. There are sales figures of every kind and detailed information about demographics, but there is very little publicly available information about how and why people start drinking wine, what they drink when they do start, and what happens next. If they start with cheap wine, do they trade up to expensive wine? If they start with sweet wine, do they eventually move to dry wine? If they start with red, do they eventually include white (or vice versa)? No one knows for sure — or, if they do, they aren't doing much with the information. Contrast this with the auto business, which knows almost exactly what the consumer is thinking from the minute they get an inkling they want to buy a new car through every step in the process. The reason for the difference is obvious. The car business has difficulty selling cars unless it understands its customers, something that isn't a problem for the wine business. Thank you, three-tier system.

Yet ask anyone in the wine business, and they're convinced that this gateway wine exists, and they can cite example after example. It was supposed to be white zinfandel in the 1990s, but every indication is that white zinfandel drinkers never did anything but drink white zinfandel, and that the decline in white zinfandel sales over the past several years is its audience dying off or getting bored, but not from trading up to dry wine. YellowTail, the cheap

Australian import, was going to be the gateway wine at the turn of the century, but that never happened, either. YellowTail found a profitable niche appealing to consumers who wanted a sound wine made in a certain style that didn't cost a lot of money, but that's all they wanted and they never seemed interested in anything else. Even YellowTail couldn't trade them up. Its line of "reserve" wines, introduced a couple of years ago to do just that, has met with mixed success.

This time around, sweet wine — in the form of the white moscato and red blends — is the gateway. No less an authority than NPR has said so, and there seems to be good reason to agree. Sweet wine appeals to non-white and younger consumers, two groups that the wine business does a poor job of reaching. For the most part, each are inexpensive and simple, without a lot of jargon attached to them. Those are key requirements for a gateway, which must not have what are called extensive barriers to entry, and high price and winespeak are two such barriers. If someone has to pay a lot of money for a product they don't understand, they won't buy it. Meanwhile, sales of moscato and sweet red have skyrocketed over the past couple of years. So, maybe, this is it?

Probably not. Moscato sales may have peaked in 2012, and there has been a chronic shortage of the moscato grape used to make the wine as well. Sweet red, says a Nielsen expert, though continuing to grow, isn't apparently bringing in new consumers. Rather, most of the growth seems to be from non-sweet drinkers shifting to sweet and sweet drinkers drinking more sweet wine.

That's because the gateway wine, as the wine business understands it, probably doesn't exist. Wine isn't marketed to people who don't drink wine, in the way that soft drinks or beer is marketed to non-soft drink and non-beer drinkers. Mountain Dew was once an almost forgotten 7-Up knockoff until someone decided to re-invigorate the brand by pitching it to 20-something men, turning into Pepi's hip and groovy younger brother. That's something the wine industry doesn't seem interested in doing. It's stuck on the affordable luxury approach, so there's no need to say, "Drink this and it will introduce you to the joys of wine," the way an auto dealer knows how to sell a young woman her first car. In fact, in all my time writing about wine, I don't know that anyone has ever asked me that question. (If they do, the answer is rose.) That they don't ask says all anyone needs to know about the subject. They don't ask because they don't think they're supposed to ask, and they don't want to ask because they're scared and intimidated by wine. It's like asking a nuclear engineer to recommend an introductory book about cold fusion. What's the point of asking a question that, even if there was an answer, they wouldn't understand?

The common thread in all of this are the questions posed in this chapter and elsewhere in the book, the questions that wine drinkers must have answers for if they are to learn to appreciate and to enjoy wine. They're not difficult questions: What's wrong with drinking cheap wine? Why won't you explain wine to me in language that I understand? Why are there so many rules? Why am I somehow inferior to you if I don't obey the rules? Why don't people who drink beer have to put up with all this stuff?

Because, when they don't get answers to their questions, they drink something else. That's their loss, certainly, because then they'll never get a chance to know wine and to share it, to taste something for the first time and to know that this is a damn fine thing to be drinking at this moment and that it's almost unbelievable how it makes the moment seem more than that. It's an almost impossible feeling to explain — you just know it, for no real reason, and accept it because it's wine and that's how wine works. It can happen anywhere, at the dinner table or at the beach, on a backyard patio or in a hotel bar, and it can happen with anyone else or with no one else. Most importantly, it can happen with cheap wine, because the moment and the feeling aren't about what a wine costs but about the wine and how it affects you.

And that it happens at all is enough to make the rest of the junk about wine, the winespeak and the foolish rules and the elitism, worth putting up with.

But it's wine's loss as well, and this has nothing to do with money or profit or market share or per capita consumption or demographics or any of the other metrics and markers that get all of the attention. Instead, it's about that moment, and that not enough people will get to experience the feeling and the moment because wine doesn't do enough to help them get there. What's the point of giving the world something wonderful when too much of what you do denies them the chance to experience that wonder? In this, a sin of omission is no different that a sin of commission, because then it is about money and profit and market share and per capita consumption and demographics, and makes wine no different from selling widgets. And wine should be — wine is — better than widgets.

Or, as Ernest Hemingway wrote in *For Whom the Bell Tolls*: "The wine was good, tasting faintly resinous from the wineskin, but excellent, light and clean on his tongue. Robert Jordan drank it slowly, feeling it spread warmly through his tiredness."

Everyone should have a moment like that.

Other good stuff to know

Winespeak dictionary

Artisan wine: Term used by multi-national producers and some small, high-end wineries to convince consumers that their labels are not made the same way as their other wines—though they often are. See **Hand-crafted wine**.

Balance: All wines, regardless of cost, should strive for balance between the various components—fruit, alcohol, acid, tannins, and oak. Well-made wines achieve balance, regardless of cost.

Blended wines: Wine made with more than one grape and called by a proprietary name. Some of the world's great wines are blends, and cheap blends often provide great quality and value.

Cheap wine: The greatest wine term in the world. Honest. Refers to wines that cost $10 or less and offer value and quality.

Corked: Wine flaw that doesn't mean the wine has bits of cork in it. Rather, the wine has been contaminated by a chemical that makes it smell like a wet basement or a wet dog and masks its true flavor and aroma. Safe to drink, but not very tasty. See **Wine flaw**.

Descriptors: Terms used to describe what a wine tastes, smells, and looks like and where the goal seems to be to confuse consumers as much as possible See **Winestream Media**. See **Winespeak**. See **Tasting notes**.

Finish: The taste and feeling in your mouth after you swallow wine. A well-made wine usually has a finish that you can taste for many seconds after swallowing.

Fruit-forward: Wines that emphasize fruitiness more than any other characteristic, where the fruit is usually the first flavor you taste. See **Fruity**.

Fruity: Wine with lots of fruit flavor, but not necessarily sweet. The fruit flavors occur naturally, and not from additives. See **Residual sugar**.

Grocery store wine: Cheap wine that usually carries a clever name and cute label (often produced by the biggest wine companies) but is often not very interesting in taste. It's important to note that not all wine sold in grocery stores is grocery store wine, and that not all grocery store wine is boring and dull. See **Plonk**.

Hand-crafted wine: How all wine is made, since no one has yet figured out how to use a machine to make wine. Term is used by some producers to imply their wine is of higher quality. See **Artisan wine**.

Hot: A wine where the alcohol content is out of balance and overpowers the other characteristics. Heat can be detected in the back of the mouth and in throat in the way whiskey tastes hot.

Minerality: Descriptor for a mineral-like flavor in the wine. Usually found in white or rose wines. See **Descriptor**.

Negociant: French term describing a company that sells wine under its own label, but doesn't necessarily make the wine or grow the grapes. Might buy grapes or even finished wine and then re-label it. Negociants are more common in the wine business than most consumers realize, and are not necessarily a bad thing.

Oxidized: Wine that has had too much exposure to oxygen and goes off, in the way a peeled apple turns brown. Usually tastes old or even like bad brandy. See **Corked**. See **Wine flaw**.

Palate: A wine geek term that refers to someone's ability to taste wine. If you have a good palate, you are better able to tell the differences between styles and kinds of wines. Someone with a bad palate often recommends wine that no one else would want to drink.

Plonk: Old-fashioned English wine term used to describe cheap and poorly made wine that was usually made in France. Often used by upper classes to describe wine they considered beneath them. See **Grocery store wine**.

Porch wine: Wine that is best enjoyed on a porch on a fine day—roses, light reds, and whites. Can even be sparkling.

Private label: Wine made for specific retailers, like Trader Joe's Two-buck Chuck, and not available anywhere. These wines are generally less expensive, and have helped keep wine prices low over the past decade. Retailers like them because they're more profitable.

Regional wine: Wine made in the 47 states that aren't California, Washington, and Oregon, and is usually frowned on by the Winestream Media.

Reserve: Term used by producers to signify a higher-quality wine when it actually has no legal meaning outside of a few European countries. When correctly used, reserve means a step up from the winery's regular wines, which doesn't apply to most of the $20 grocery store bottles that it does show up on.

Residual sugar: How sweet the wine actually is, based on the amount of sugar left over after fermentation (or the amount of sugar or sugar-like ingredients, including grape juice concentrate that the winery adds). Usually a closely guarded secret. See **Fruity**.

Room temperature: A wine term left over from the 19th century that suggested the temperature for serving wine. However, since it referred to the temperature of a room in western Europe before air conditioning or central heat, it's irrelevant today. Suggested serving temperature for red wine is 60-65 degrees F (15-18 C) and 50-55 degrees F (10-13 C) for whites. In the U.S., we tend to serve reds in the mid- to upper-70s and whites at 35, which is refrigerator temperature.

Sommelier: Someone who oversees wine service in a higher-end restaurant and may have been certified as master of wine or master sommelier. Many sommeliers are experts who can help choose wine, but a title or initials after a name does not guarantee expertise.

Suggested retail price: The price suggested by the producer, usually higher than the price on store shelves. One rule of thumb:

The street price is $2 or $3 less than the suggested price, so a $12.99 wine may sell for as little for $10.

Sulfites: Chemicals that include sulfur dioxide and that occur naturally in wine and many other foods, including shredded coconut and dried apricots (the latter of which has 10 times the sulfites of most wines). Winemakers add sulfites to help wine age, enhance the color, and retard bacterial growth, and white wines usually have more sulfites than reds.

Tannins: Chemical that comes come from grape skins, as well as the seeds and the stems, that gives wine an astringent or puckery feeling in the mouth. Red wine is more tannic than white, since white rarely uses skins in winemaking. There are tannins in sweet red wine. There aren't as noticeable because the sugar covers up the tannins.

Tasting notes: Wine writing that uses descriptors linked together to describe specific wines, and is often as difficult to understand as a foreign language. See **Descriptors**. See **Winespeak**.

Terroir: French wine term that doesn't have an exact English translation, but is usually defined as "of the soil." In most limited sense, means the actual soil the grapes grew in, as in the *terroir* of a vineyard. In larger, more philosophical sense, means the history, tradition, and technical background of a region, as in the *terroir* of left bank of Bordeaux.

Three-tier system: The wine distribution system that limits consumers to buying wine from retailers and restaurants, and forces them to actually go into the store to purchase it. Three-tier is protected by the U.S. Constitution, just like freedom of speech and religion.

Varietal: The name of the grape used to make the wine, like chardonnay or cabernet sauvignon. One of the most important moments in cheap wine history came in the 1980s, when California producers decided to focus on varietal wine instead of blends.

Varietal wines: Wines made of just one varietal, though U.S law allows other grapes to be blended and for it be called a varietal wine.

Vinifera: The species of grape that generally is easiest to turn into high-quality wine, like chardonnay and cabernet sauvignon.

Vintage: The year the grapes used to make the wine were harvested. Vintage, for 90 percent of the wine we drink, means very little, since these wines are made to taste the same every year.

Wine flaw: Problem with the wine cause by poor winemaking or inadequate storage after winemaking. Flawed wines are usually obvious from the taste or smell. See **Corked**. See **Oxidized**.

Winespeak: Opaque and confusing language used by Winstream Media and its allies in wine discussions, reviews, and tasting notes that makes it difficult for others to understand what they're saying. By this, it establishes itself as the arbiters of wine taste.

Winestream Media: The handful of wine magazines and top critics who feel their job is to tell the rest of us what to drink — and if we don't believe them, we obviously know nothing about wine. See **Winespeak**.

Green wine: Making sense of organic, bio-dynamic, and sustainably farmed

The market for organic products in the United States has grown more than 25-fold in the last two decades. Somehow, though, wine made with organic methods hasn't shared in this growth. There are green wines, of course, but they're a tiny part of the market and wine drinkers have shown little enthusiasm for them, and certainly not in the way grocery shoppers have flocked to organic products. You can see this yourself—compare the size of the organic vegetable department at your local grocer with the green wine section at your wine shop.

There are three reasons for this: First, it's not easy to decipher the terminology. An organic wine is not, technically, the same thing as an organic tomato. A tomato is either organic or it isn't; wine falls into one of four categories, only one of which is similar to the traditional definition of organic. Wine can be green if it's:

- Made with organic grapes. These wines are similar to the organic tomato, since the grapes used to make the wine must be grown according to federal regulations and will be labeled as such. This method, though, doesn't guarantee that other parts of the winemaking process, like wood barrels used for aging, are organic.

- Labeled organic. This has nothing to do with the grapes, but signifies that the wine was made without added sulfites. Sulfites, which occur naturally in all wine, act as a preservative, and winemakers usually add more to the wine during fermentation. This is also regulated by the federal government, and the label will say organic.

- Bio-dynamic. The next step beyond organic, based on principles established by European philosopher Rudolf Steiner almost 100 years ago. It includes guidelines for crop diversity and planting, and can be quite practical. But its bio-dynamic's aesthetic side that has garnered the most attention, for bio-dynamic farming takes in a "spiritual-ethical-ecological approach to agriculture, food production and nutrition." Certified by the private Demeter Institute and usually labeled as such.

- Sustainably farmed. This is the newest certification, part of a project by the Wine Institute trade group and the California Association of Winegrape Growers. They established the California Sustainable Winegrowing Alliance in 2003, and wine done this way has a sustainable label. The group calls for growers and wineries to use "vineyard and winery practices that are sensitive to the environment, responsive to the needs and interests of society-at-large, and economically feasible to implement and maintain." Make of that what you will in terms of how green the wines are.

Second, no one has quite figured out whether eco-friendly wines taste better than conventional wines, in the way that organic tomatoes usually taste fresher and more tomato-like than conventional tomatoes. Much of this is the nature of winemaking, in which the product is manipulated and processed in a way that tomatoes aren't. Pick an organic tomato, and you can eat it immediately. Pick a grape grown with green methods, and you'll have to wait at least a year until you can drink the wine. That contradiction is telling. There is also an argument, as proposed by Dave McIntyre of the Washington Post, that this kind of natural winemaking "can be an excuse for bad winemaking." His point is that many of the practices used in modern winemaking, like adding sulfites, have improved the quality of wine. Do without, and we could well be back in the 19th century.

Third, green wines confuse people who sell wine. They inhabit a no-man's-land at many retailers, where they're found mostly in organic sections set off from the rest of the wine in the same nether reaches of the store as boxed wine and wine from local and regional producers (even in stores that focus on other green products). There are no nationally-distributed green wines in the way brands like Kendall-Jackson are nationally distributed. Bonterra, one of the best known eco-friendly labels, sold 300,000 cases in 2012 — a lot of wine, but nothing to rank it among the best sellers. The best known bio-dynamically produced wine is Bonny Doon, which is about as close to a cult producer in terms of production as a company can be whose wines don't fetch $100.

Ironically, despite the buildup in the rest of retailing this century, green is nothing new to the wine business. Bio-dynamic farming is almost 100 years old, the Romans and Greeks made wine with organic grapes, and even the European wine business was mostly organic until chemical pesticides, herbicides, and fertilizers were invented in the last century. What's new is the emphasis on these practices, part of the slow food and local food movements of the past decade. A 2007 survey by The Hartman Group found that more than three-quarters of respondents said "it's important to buy environmentally friendly products" and that they were nearly four times as likely to pay a 10 percent premium for sustainable products.

Despite this, eco-friendly wines aren't necessarily more expensive than their conventional counterparts, a stark contrast to other organic products, where an organic tomato may cost 10 percent or more than a conventional tomato. There are several reasons for this; probably the most important is that the wholesale market for organic grapes isn't mature enough to support a price premium, says Cliff Bingham of Bingham Family Vineyards in West Texas, who has raised organic grapes but now farms them conventionally.

The contrast to the demand for Bingham's organic crops, including cotton and peanuts, is telling and speaks to not just the market for organic grapes from producers, but from consumers. Shoppers want organic peanut butter, but just aren't interested in organic wine.

Why wine scores are useless, and how they're used to trick you

Hedges CMS White is a quality $10 wine, a sauvignon blanc blend from Washington state that offers consistent value from vintage to vintage. It's not fancy, but it's not supposed to be; rather, it's the kind of wine to drink when you want a glass but don't want to make a fuss. It's also the perfect example of everything that's wrong with wine scores.

Wine scores are ratings given to wine, usually on a 100-point scale. Robert Parker, for much of the last 30 years the most powerful wine critic in the world, made scores the most popular way to evaluate wine and his legacy is everywhere—in reviews on blogs and websites, in the high-end wine magazines, and even in newspapers; on winery websites and in winery publicity materials; and in almost every store that sells wine, highlighted on the shelf talkers clipped to the shelf under the wine. An entire generation of wine drinkers has been corrupted by scores, afraid to buy anything that hasn't received a high mark or to try something just because they want to try it.

Witness the Hedges. CellarTracker is an on-line wine inventory app that allows wine drinkers to record what they buy and drink, and to write public tasting notes that include scores. One recent vintage of the Hedges—which tasted pretty much the same as always — got scores ranging from 77 to 90 from CellarTracker users. How did people, drinking the exact same wine, come to almost completely different conclusions about its quality? Because, as has been reiterated time and time again on these pages, everyone's palate is different, and what one person likes may not be what another person likes. Which means the concept behind scores, that one person can rate a wine for others, is flawed from the start.

But that's only the beginning of why scores don't work:

- Reviewer bias. A critic who doesn't like merlot or riesling is less likely to give those wines a high score.
- Red wine bias. Red wines score higher than white wines, because red wines are considered more important than white wines. I recently asked a colleague to help me do a double-blind, academic study to demonstrate this, but he said it wasn't necessary: "Everyone already knows this is true," he said.
- Cheap wine bias. A $100 wine is more likely to get a better score than a $10 wine, even if it isn't better, because its price means it's a more important wine and deserves a better score.
- Score inflation. Theoretically, scores are similar to the 100-point school grading system, so a 95-point wine is a solid A, a 90-point wine is an A-minus, and so forth. But, over the past decade, it has become increasingly rare for wines to receive scores lower than 85. In one respect, this speaks to the improved quality of all wine, but it also demonstrates that critics are reluctant (for whatever reason) to be too harsh. Which raises the question: What's the point of a system that doesn't mark down or fail wines that deserve it? What other criticism — film, restaurants, TV — works that way?

At best, scores are lazy, because they don't tell the consumer enough about the wine. This is something Eric Asimov of the New York Times noted in 2011: Scores, he told a wine bloggers conference, may work in the context of retailing. But add food, mood, and people to the mix and scores becomes meaningless. At worst, scores are dishonest, because they play to the wine industry's elitism, reinforcing the idea that consumers don't know enough about wine to make their own decisions and that they need an expert to guide them. Can anyone imagine this happening with film criticism? Hollywood would go out of business after just one summer of critically-panned blockbusters.

Good critics, in any field, give their audience enough information to make up his or her own mind. The best critics are conduits, placing the wine in perspective — Asimov's food, mood, and people. And the best critics facilitate discussion, understanding that they are not the final arbiter but one voice among many. In this, they should be an intelligent, well-versed, and thoughtful voice that consumers can learn from, and it should be enough that they describe what the wine tastes like, whether they thought it was well made, and how it pairs with food.

Nevertheless, scores have thrived in the past three decades because they sell wine. Even better, they do it on the cheap. Retailers don't need an employee to move a Parker 95 or a Wine Spectator 94. All they need to do is to clip a shelf talker in the appropriate place and the wine practically sells itself. Or, as one retailer told me several years ago, "We can't hand sell every customer."

But that's not the only example of the system's insidiousness. Distributors use scores to sell wine to retailers and restaurants in the same way, because time saved is money earned. Otherwise, the distributor has to explain the wine to the store owner during the sales call, and who wants to go through that when it's easier and even more effective to give them a promotion sheet that says Wine Enthusiast 93? Even worse is that scores are used by wineries and distributors to influence other critics, on the theory that someone won't write badly about a wine that has already earned a 92. The loser in every case is the consumer, who may end up buying a wine for no other reason than someone they know nothing about gave it a good score for reasons they don't understand.

The irony about scores is that Parker intended them to improve wine criticism. In those long ago days, wine writing was dominated by Europeans who wrote less about what the wine tasted like and more about the wine tasting experience as part of the 500 years of the European wine tradition. David Michalski, in a penetrating 2013 essay tracing the growth of California wine, saw this as crucial to what has happened since. Parker's "consumer advocacy," he wrote, "powered by his system of awarding numeric scores to wines he tasted blind, also sought to liberate the wine industry from the outworn traditionalist biases of high-end wine merchants and auction-house critics."

Yet the revolution always devours its children, and scores are today's traditions, championed by the 21st century version of those merchants and auction-house critics. Consumers want scores, say the traditionalists, so we must use them, ignoring the chicken and egg fallacy. Scores were never meant to be objective, they claim, ignoring that scores have always been presented as the final word. Or, most ingenuously they argue, scores work, ignoring that they don't work for the people who are supposed to benefit, but for the people who give the scores.

The future of wine won't have scores in it, if for no other reason than wine drinkers raised on scores are dying off, and the next generations will likely see scores as quaint as turntables or those football-sized 1980s car phones. But scores will also fall away because wine is being democratized, and who needs someone you don't know to tell you if a wine is worth drinking when you know enough to make up your own mind?

How to buy wine for dinner

Two scenes over the last several years illustrate everything about the wine business that makes it so difficult to buy wine, and why so many people give up and drink Dr Pepper. In one, a youngish man stared helplessly at an employee in a long-time Dallas liquor store and all but begged for advice on "buying wine for pasta," and the employee didn't quite know what to do. The other came more recently, at a national retailer famous for cheap wine and its 20- and 30-something women customers.

20-something woman: "I need to buy some wine for a party."

Store employee: "We have this wonderful pinot noir, great scores, won a gold medal."

20-something woman: "Do you have something that costs $8 a bottle?"

In each case, the customer wanted to buy wine that was professionally made at a fair price, but had no idea how to do it. When someone needs help to buy a cheap bottle of Italian red wine to have with spaghetti, we're all in trouble.

But it doesn't have to be confusing or unpleasant. Buying wine for dinner can be fun, and you shouldn't have to approach it with the same enthusiasm you bring to mopping the floor. Yes, it's better if you have a trusted retailer (see Chapter IV), but it's not essential. It's possible to go to the store, including the grocery

store, and buy quality cheap wine for dinner — even on the spur
of the moment or on the way home from work.

Keep these tips in mind:

- Keep it simple. Too many wine buyers think too much
about what they should buy, and all that does is compli-
cate matters. Unless you're having the boss to dinner, don't
worry about layered flavors and nuances and all the rest of
the eye-glazing winespeak (and there's even an argument
that it doesn't matter with the boss). It won't make any
difference on a Tuesday night when all you want is a glass
of wine with the roast chicken you're also going to buy at
the grocery store. In most cases, a less tannic, fruity red or
white is sufficient.

- Boxed wine. The problem with three-liter boxed wine is
not the box that it comes in (unless you're a wine snob, in
which case you're probably not reading this), but the annoying inconsistency of the quality of the wine. When it's
right, boxed wine is the answer to every mid-week dinner.
Keep it in the refrigerator, open the spigot, and you're set. It
lasts almost forever, and won't spoil after the seal has been
broken. The catch is the quality, since boxed wine is made
to hit a price point and not necessarily to be consistent
from vintage to vintage. That means that if grapes are more
expensive one year, the producer has to use cheaper grapes,
which usually translates into poorer quality grapes. Having
said that, producers like Black Box and Maipe are your best
bets.

- Buy wine that you know you like, but from a different
producer. One of the worst habits wine drinkers get into is
buying the same wine over and over (and over and over).
Again, this is understandable, but there's no need for it. If
you like chardonnay from Kendall-Jackson or another big

producer, try chardonnay from a different and perhaps less known winery that costs about the same price. You'll be surprised at how quickly this technique helps you learn more about wine.

- Buy wine that you know you like, but from a different region. If you like Australian shiraz, then try a French syrah from the Rhone that costs about the same price. They won't taste exactly like each other, but that's the point, isn't it? Plus, you'll get to impress everyone with your newly acquired wine knowledge of grapes and regions.

- Sparkling wine or rose (as discussed in Chapter V). The former will add a smile, literally, to almost any Chinese takeout, because who would have the audacity to drink sparkling wine with fried rice or moo shu pork? The latter is one of the most neglected wines on store shelves, and for no good reason. Both also deliver more than $10 worth of wine for their usual $10 price tag.

The one thing you don't have to worry about? Food and wine pairings. You can if you want, but it's not necessary (as discussed in Chapter V). Yes, there is good reason for pairing red wine with meat and white wine with chicken and fish, but if you don't like big, tannic red wines or crisp, fruity whites, don't buy one just for the pairing. No matter how well made the wine is or how many wine critics gush over its affinity with steak, it's not going to help you enjoy dinner if you want to spit it out after the first sip.

Regional wine and why it matters

The fastest growing part of the U.S. wine business isn't in California, Washington, or Oregon, and it's not about wine scores or cult wines. It's just the opposite — it's wine made in the other 47 states and that is rarely critically acclaimed or lusted after by wine geeks. It's called regional wine or local wine or even locapour, and this development may be as revolutionary as the advances in viticulture and winemaking technology were over the past couple of decades.

Today, wine is made in all 50 states, including Alaska and Hawaii. The number of regional wineries — those that aren't in California, Oregon and Washington — has grown 10-fold since 1975. Though California still produces about 90 percent of the wine made in the U.S., there were some 3,500 wineries in the other 47 states in 2012, about the same number as California. Texas, New York and Virginia combined have about 1,000 wineries, to say nothing of 202 in Ohio, 135 in Illinois and a dozen or so in Alaska.

This change is about more than numbers, because it points to a change in attitude. It signals that wine drinkers are willing to try something that doesn't come with a West Coast pedigree, isn't made with grapes that they're familiar with, and doesn't have a Winestream Media seal of approval. This is revolutionary, given the parochial nature of the wine business before the beginning of the 21st century, when wine had to be what other people who knew more about wine said it was. And regional wine was derided as crappy and sweet, made with unworthy grapes by amateurs. The only thing it was good for was making fun of, as a Time magazine article in 2008 did, complete with snarkiness and inaccuracy. In this, the growth in local wine has mirrored that of cheap wine, as wine drinkers have increasingly made up their own minds about what to drink.

This infuriates the Winestream Media, which sees the rise of regional wine as a direct challenge to its authority in a way not even cheap wine has been. Or, as one writer told me during a long and heated late-night discussion: "What's the point? Why do we need it?" That he even had to ask the question demonstrates how little he understands what's going on. That's not his question to ask any more.

This is not to say that regional wine is as accomplished as California wine and that there isn't room for improvement. Quality remains annoyingly inconsistent, thanks to a lack of resources — money, education, and qualified employees. Price has traditionally been a problem, since regional wineries are too small to benefit from economies of scale and must charge more for their product. Fortunately, as regional wine grows, this is becoming less of an issue, and there is more and more tasty $10 regional wine available. Grapes, both in quantity and quality, have also been not been up to California's standards, though that is starting to change as well.

Local wine still suffers from image problems, and this may be the last obstacle standing in the way of mainstream acceptance. Too many people who should know better, including those in the wine and restaurant businesses, treat local as if it was still 1975. The local food movement has been slow to embrace local wine, despite what seem like similar agendas. And too many consumers, even younger ones, still see it as somehow inferior, and they don't have to taste it to know that's true. They've been taught that all wine should taste like it comes from California and should be made with the same grapes. So when a regional winery makes something from a lesser known European-style grape, or, even worse, from a native grape or a hybrid, they just know it can't be any good.

Regional producers made this problem worse in the early days when they made chardonnay, merlot, and cabernet sauvignon even though their *terroir* wasn't suited for it. They made them because consumers knew what they were and would buy them, and that cash flow was crucial to staying in business. That was the case in Texas for years, when growers struggled with the classic grapes despite a climate that was too hot, too dry, and too full of pests. Hence a lot of chardonnay that was barely drinkable, even on its best days, and that Texas is still trying to live down.

Yet, having said all this, the best regional wine from the leading states — Texas, New York, Virginia, and Missouri at least — is a match for anything in the rest of the world, both in quality and value. New Mexico's Gruet Winery has been so successful with its $15 sparkling wine that it ran out of New Mexico grapes years ago, and today supplements its local fruit with grapes it buys on the West Coast. Rieslings from New York's Finger Lakes are some of the world's best, and leading English wine writers regularly rave about Virginia's red blends.

But quality is not local's only attribute. Regional wine doesn't taste like California wine or French wine. It tastes like the region it came from, and that's something great wine is supposed to do. Taste a New York wine, and it's different from California and France, but also from Virginia. It's so frustrating that the Winestream Media fell all over itself embracing Australia's unique style of shiraz a decade ago, yet never seemed the least bit interested in granting that privilege to regional wine.

Regional wine, in fact, may well lead to the thing that the wine business fears most — democratization, in which consumers drink whatever they like from wherever they like, without interference from the Winestream Media, wine retailers and distributors, Big Wine, and the three-tier system. Every person who buys an Indiana traminette or a Missouri chambourcin or a New York baco noir is reducing the power and the importance of the oligarchies that have run the wine business in the United States for 40 years.

And wouldn't that be a good thing?

Acknowledgments

This book has been in the works for almost 20 years, even when I didn't know that it was. That means there are dozens and dozens of people to thank — and that doesn't include all of those who, given their role in the wine business and what I've written here, hope I don't thank them. They've got jobs to keep, after all. All I can do is mention those who, for better or worse, put me on this path.

In this, I am responsible for what is in these pages. The opinions are my own, based on my 30 years of drinking, reporting, and writing about wine, and I am responsible for what is written here.

My wine writing career would not have been possible without Dianne Teitelbaum, who answered every question I asked her all those years ago and never once told me I was too stupid to figure this thing out. Amy Culbertson, the former food editor at the Star-Telegram newspaper in Fort Worth, gave me this nickname and a place to begin my campaign to demystify wine. Cathy Frisinger, formerly of the Star-Telegram, also trusted my judgment.

John Bratcher, The Other Wine Guy, has always been patient and understanding, even when I was especially curmudgeonly. Much of what is written here has been distilled through his knowledge and good sense in our years spent together talking and drinking wine. Paul Gerald, the guru of self-publishing, showed someone who started with typewriters and carbon paper in the newspaper business what was possible with 21st century book publishing technology. My wine colleagues and friends, including Dave McIntyre, Doug Caskey, Michael Wangbickler, Kyle Schlachter, Robert Whitley, James Tidwell, Alfonso Cevola, and

Hunter Hammett, were generous with their time and wisdom, answering questions and offering advice. My brother, Jim, pushed me to write the book when I thought it wasn't possible or necessary. George Taber patiently explained how the publishing business had changed since my last book, and why that mattered to me. Tim McNally read the manuscript and stopped me from writing more than one thing I shouldn't have written. Jenny Gregorcyk and Denise Clarke are always ready with marketing and public relations wisdom, two things I always need help with.

Rick Rockwell edited the book with a firm hand and a much appreciated perspective, offering professional insight, a sounding board for my rants and complaints, and much-needed encouragement. I just hope I wasn't as difficult to work with as those local TV anchors he used to supervise.

Jennifer Omner guided me through the post-modern world of ebooks and digital layout, and made the ebook and print books look as good as they do. Jynette Neal designed the cover (amazing, yes?) and did much of the graphics and chart work. Bob Smith's work on the printing end was exemplary, and he made sure I understood everything that was involved.

The 113 people who backed my campaign on Kickstarter, which paid for the design, layout, and printing of the book, demonstrated the power of crowd funding. It was truly amazing, to say nothing of gratifying, to see people who knew me only as a digital voice on the Internet support the book, and I appreciate their faith and foresight. Crowd funding and crowd sourcing may well be the future of book publishing, and I'm glad I was able to part of it.

Finally, Lynne Kleinpeter introduced me to wine when I was a nothing more than a beer-drinking sportswriter who thought wine was something other people drank. That's just one of the millions of things she has done for me since then, and that I appreciate more than she will ever know — or believe.